Nigel Lambourne

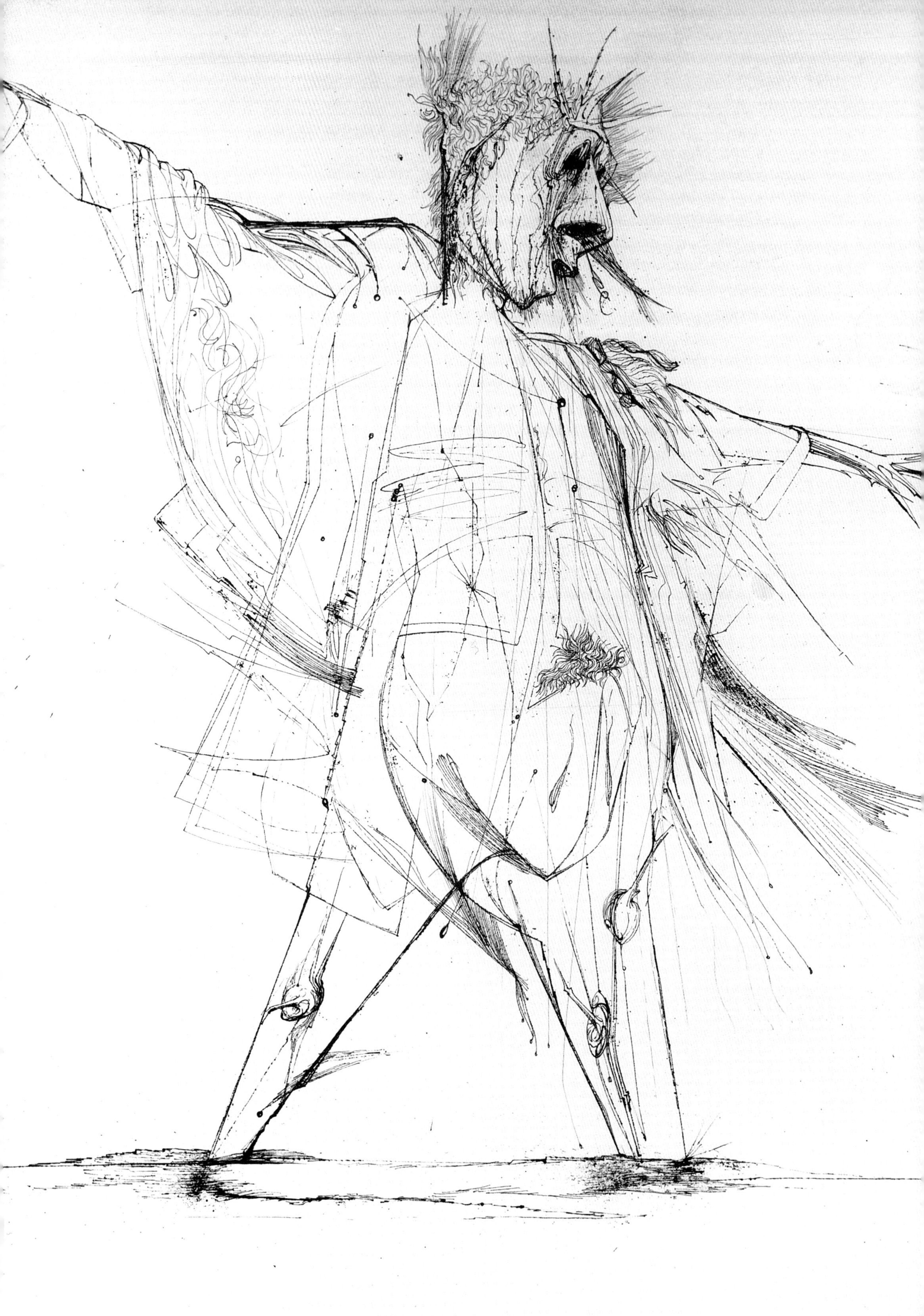

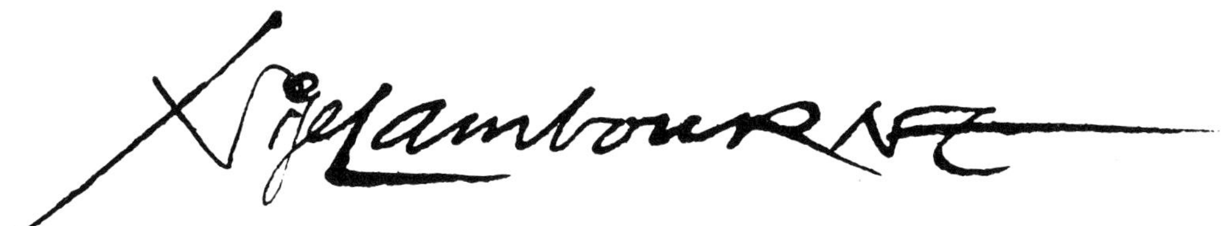

draughtsman, printmaker, illustrator 1919-1988

DOUGLAS MARTIN

VICTORIA ART GALLERY, BATH

4 APRIL – 16 MAY 1992

First published in 1992 by the
Victoria Art Gallery, Bath City Council
Bridge Street, Bath BA2 4AT

ISBN 0-901303-27-5

A CIP catalogue record for this book is available from the British Library

Designed by Douglas Martin Associates
Phototypeset in Janson Dutch Old Style
by Armitage Typo/Graphics Ltd, Huddersfield
Printed and bound in Great Britain
by Barwell Colour Print, Bath

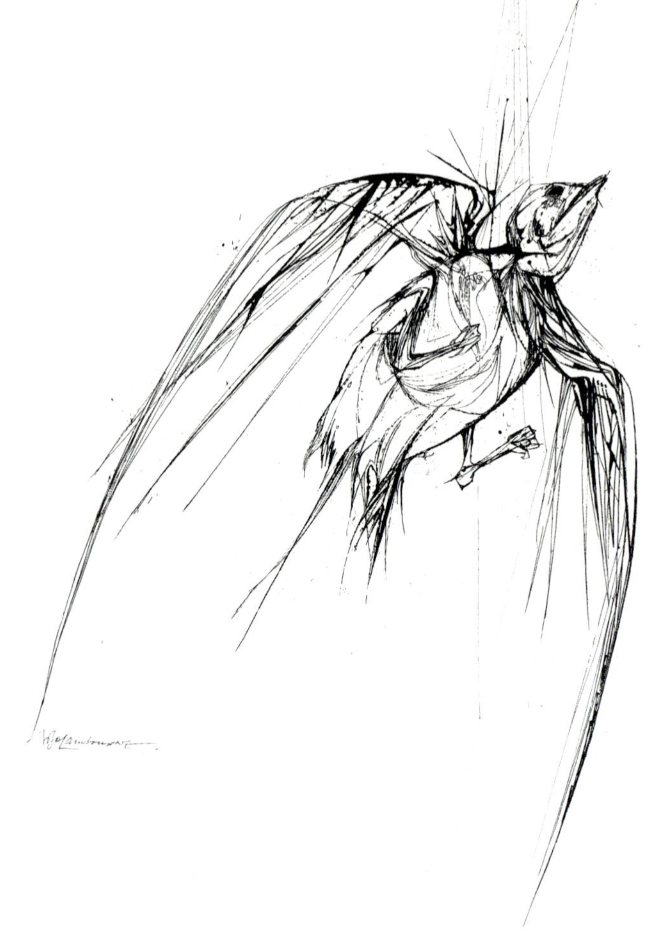

[No.46] *Bird Image*, late 1960s

Front cover: [No. 7] *Bullfight VI*, c.1950
Back cover: [No. 5] *The Financial Body*, 1950 or earlier
Frontispiece: [No. 40] *Scarecrow Image*, 1968

Acknowledgements

This is the first major exhibition of the work of Nigel Lambourne to be held in over thirty years. Lambourne's work is not widely known today, yet during the 1950s he received great critical acclaim. Extraordinarily, he chose to withdraw entirely from the London art scene at the height of his career, moving first to Enderby, near Leicester, where he taught part-time at the Polytechnic, and later to Oakhill, near Bath, where he spent the last four years of his life. During all this time, however, his artistic achievement continued in private.

Lambourne's exceptional talent was more than simple precision of draughtsmanship; he had an almost 'sixth sense' for line, but at the time drawing was more generally regarded as an adjunct to painting, and this was perhaps a clue to his disillusionment. In recent years there has been a renewed interest in drawing and we believe that the time has now come for a reappraisal of Nigel Lambourne's work. We are delighted that the Victoria Art Gallery can play a part in this.

We are most grateful to all those who have lent works to the exhibition for their generosity, and to the following for supplying information or photographs: The Arts Council Collection; The Folio Society; National Art Gallery, New Zealand; the National Gallery of Victoria, Melbourne, Australia; Nottingham City Museum, Castle Museum and Art Gallery; Fotek Photography, Bath; and to Henry Soden of Leicester for framing.

Many people have kindly provided advice and assistance during the preparation of this catalogue. We should like to thank in particular: David Chambers, Charles Ede, Rigby Graham, Ann Hall, Dr Nigel Vaux Halliday, Martyn Lambourne, Lowell Libson, Julia MacRae, Sue Martin, Curt Visel, and Desmond and Ann Zwemmer. I would especially like to thank Douglas Martin, not only for compiling and designing the catalogue, but also for his invaluable help and advice at every stage of the project. Above all, our thanks go to Barbara Lambourne. Without her generosity both in lending works and in giving so much of her time, it would have been impossible to hold this retrospective exhibition of Nigel Lambourne's work, so long overdue.

Victoria Barwell
Arts Officer
Victoria Art Gallery

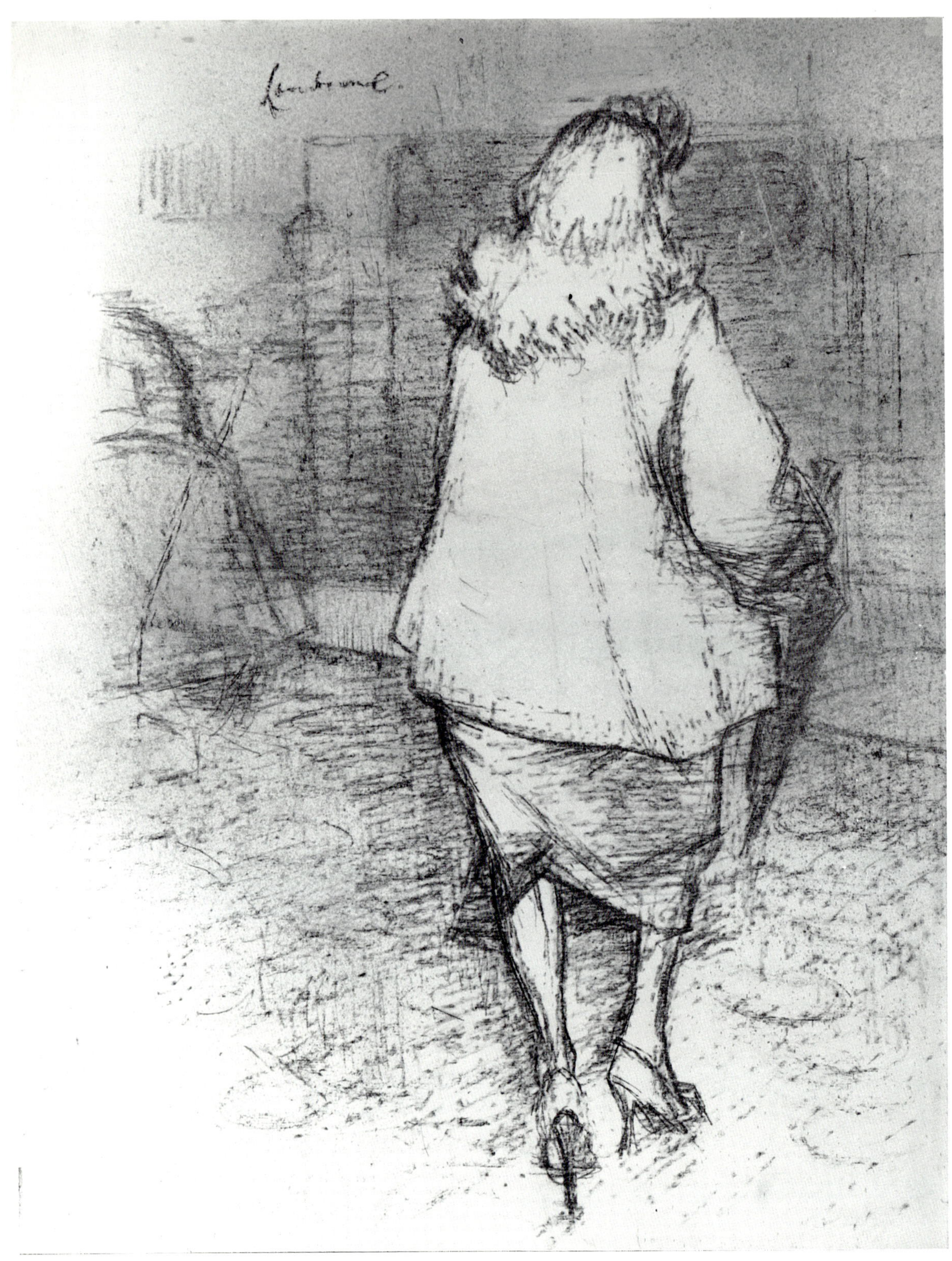

[No.4] *Streetwalker, Antwerp*, c.1949

Nigel Lambourne

I

Nigel Lambourne was a master of line. He was never greatly interested in painting. In his introduction to a selection of Renoir's work, he observed that 'Renoir was also far more conscious than most painters of his time, that there existed a peculiarly immanent quality in drawing as a language in its own right.' Lambourne sometimes referred to a sense in which painting would have come almost too easily to himself, implying that in painting there are so many ways in which it is possible to cheat when in difficulties – whereas 'the discipline of line drawing is one of the most exacting (and sometimes stultifying) techniques a painter can use'.[1] Oil pigment, with its propensity for dialogue with, and its ability to cover up for, deficiencies in draughtsmanship, is absent as a medium for his mature work. Pastel, though, as Lambourne deployed it – rather under the influence of Degas – was well adapted to the exigencies of drawing and placed colour in an ancillary role. But it was pure black and white line drawing and engraving, executed according to the rules, that represented the ultimate high-wire act for Lambourne. It was arduous and uncertain work, and he seldom expressed himself content with the outcome.

Observation from life was a starting point for him, but it also represented a quality not to be lost in working through to the final image. He could walk into a life class and produce a magnificent drawing, and there could seem to be little more to it than that on the right day. But, more than anyone I have ever met, he agonised over the gap between drawing as mere observation and reportage and achieving a finished statement. It could be exciting to be with him in a pub or restaurant when he suddenly spotted something – usually a woman across a room – that he drew your attention to in such a way that for a moment you were able to see through his eyes and to superimpose his version of a latent drawing over the living image. Barbara Lambourne makes the same point, but from a slightly different sight-line:

> I am certain that, if Nigel could freely choose where he was to live, he would say Marseille, for this city, which has been described as a city infernal and eternal, seems to be his natural home. Normally protesting if asked to walk any distance, he must have covered countless miles just idly walking through the crowded clamorous streets of this wonderful city, just for the joy of seeing and being. He has to be almost forcibly dragged from any café which commands a specially busy prospect. After all, here the women are truly women and sometimes appear to be imitating a Nigel Lambourne drawing![2]

And so, many a drawing originates from nature or the model, although, at the time, this may consist of nothing more than 'fragmentary notation of essentials before the full-scale picture was begun and worked out.'[3]

There could be numerous false starts at this working-out stage. He delighted in the simplification or the resolution of an unconventional pose or composition to a stage where it became archetypal for him. *Torso for the Sake of It*, 1986, and *Diagram of a Torso, Maybe*, 1988 (nos. 74 and 75), are fine late examples of a life drawing which has been reduced to such minimal linear terms and yet remains capable of endless variation and nuance of expression. He would return to such motifs again and again over the years, overworking an existing drawing or destroying and starting afresh. And when spring came – he always regarded this as his time for printmaking – he liked to cut or engrave or draw on stone those themes which suited one or more of the media of which he was master. To this end, the composition was already fixed and the drawing resolved, and therefore he was free to concentrate on the contrasting properties and the language of the process in question. So one often comes across versions of familiar drawings that have been translated into printmaking terms: both the white line of linocut and the incised black line in copper. Similar connections exist between drawings for book illustration and variants of the same themes from literature that were never intended for publication, but may have been re-explored out of artistic curiosity even years after the event.[4]

Lambourne's work falls into two categories; these are roughly equal in terms of his output and yet reasonably distinct in style. At the risk of over-simplification it can be said that the division is one between the kind of draughtsmanship that results from direct observation and working from the model and from life on the one hand; and on the other hand such drawings as spring directly from the inner life of the imagination. Let us turn first to the process of working out a drawing from life. Lambourne noted what this entailed for him in the case of one particular earlyish drawing, *The Corset*, but his comments would hold good for any number of similar studies.[5] Extracts have been reproduced as an extended note, since this affords an incidental and rare glimpse of Lambourne as teacher. His lucidity and integrity came as a revelation to the few; and, having taught design students alongside him, I know how stimulating and patient he could be whenever confronted by talent or application – although it could be quite another matter in the absence of both.

A number of straight life drawings which survive from all but his final period would apparently have been made direct from the model and not developed or finalised subsequently, but there are still others (i.e. the splendid *Life Study*, 1967, no. 38) about which it is impossible to be sure. For a long period in earlier days, he, Clifford Hall (1904-1973) and John Buckland-Wright (1897-1954), shared the cost of a model for their Saturday gatherings at Hall's studio;[6] but when Nigel lost contact with art colleges and their life classes after 1972 it is probable that many of his life studies were reworkings of earlier material, to which he brought great reserves of insight and intellectual revision.

The pattern of overworking – for clarity as distinct from elaboration – and then destroying and creating afresh, which can be observed in the corpus of naturalistic drawings, is even more pronounced in the case of the imaginative drawings:

> In this love-hate affair of mine with drawing – no idea exists or can exist until it is worked through-out-through. The most brilliant technique cannot do it alone. It merely looks 'brilliant'. Because it's not a sustained, utterly sustained 'throughness': an end in, and of, itself.[7]

The wastage, particularly in the later phases of Lambourne's career, must have been

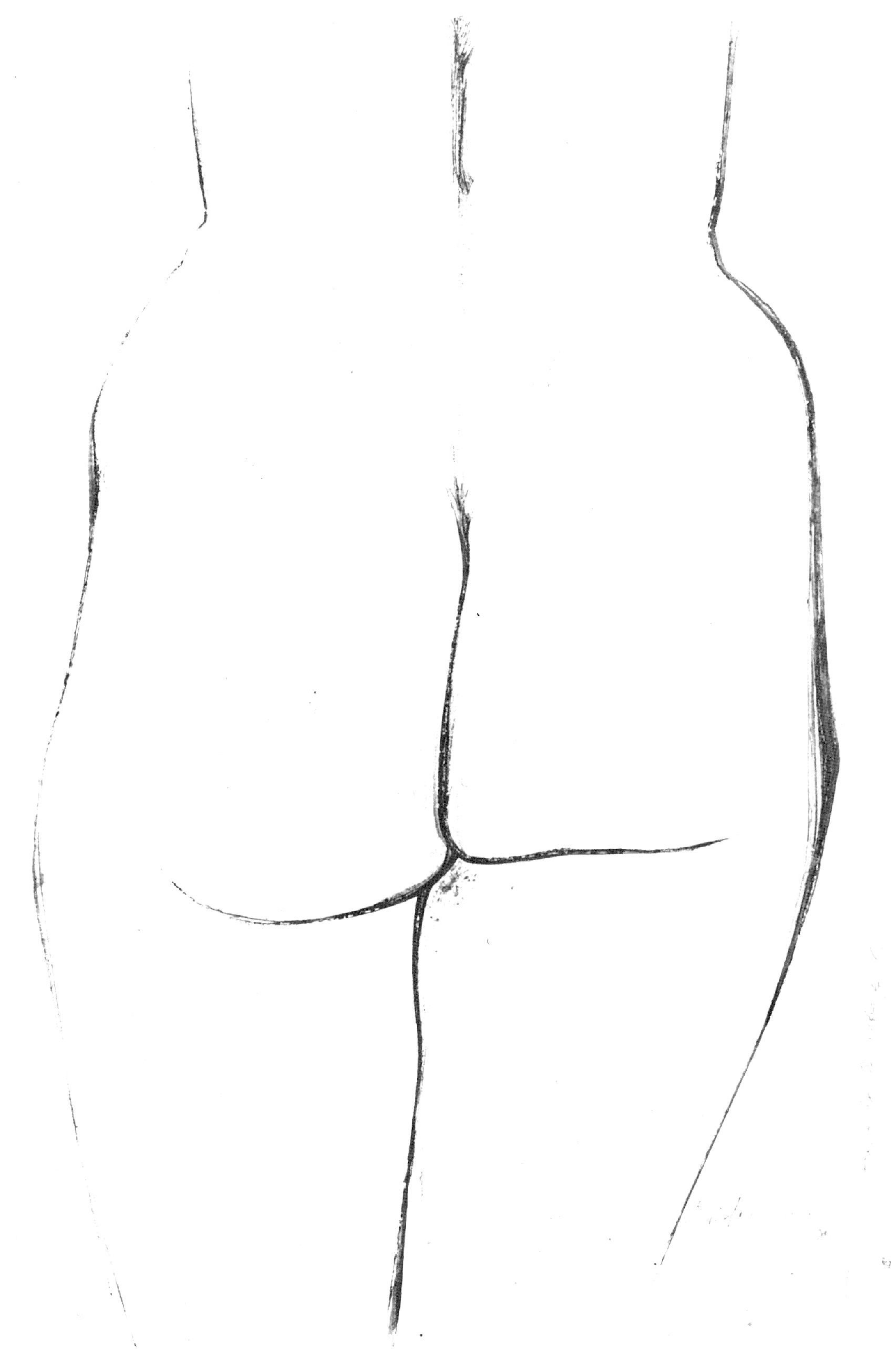

[No. 74] *Torso for the Sake of It*, 1986

horrendous. Most abortive and second-rank efforts would have been torn up on the spot, and which drawings survived his periodic siftings through plan-chests and portfolios seems to have hung very much upon the mood of the day. A cache of letters and sketches from his Royal College and Antwerp days was fortunately preserved by his close friends and fellow artists Clifford and Ann Hall. A fair number of drawings of varying quality (including most of the exceptionally fine early bullfighters and bathers), were also protected in private collections from the fate they might have met with sooner or later in Enderby or Oakhill. Of the burning days, none can have been more tragic than those which attended the removal from Enderby to the smaller cottage at Oakhill. It must have been shortly after this that he wrote to me:

> Whistler told Sickert that to destroy selectively gave one *a chance to remain* – that the best might survive. I've done *my* share of rubbishing believe me! Much disappeared *before* I truly suspected all the hidden weaknesses, long before implacable limitations began to compel me to imitate, quote myself, almost before I was half way into an idea. A kind of corrosion of course. Similar to hardened arteries?[8]

The dating of all Lambourne's extant work is perhaps not an urgent or important matter when weighed against the extreme complexity of the task, or when compared to the greater need for a record of its present whereabouts, or if set against the fact that chronology didn't matter a jot to the artist. 'Another skeletal fragment I am very much afraid. And, as usual, some dates are indeed very movable feasts.'[9] Apart from missing dates, points to note are that the current date was often added when a present or sale was made of a drawing or print; dates have been obliterated and replaced repeatedly – both at the time and subsequently; wildly differing dates occur where all the evidence points to close dates; the significance of redating and double dating is not consistent; and most prints were not properly editioned and dated. It is not that the artist is being deliberately unhelpful so much as that he seemed to wish to look on everything as work still in progress, and felt that ideally the implications of each advance he made should have retrospective effect where possible.

Chronology is further complicated because Lambourne exhibited nothing at all between 1960 and 1971, and so there is little documentary corroboration for the considerable body of work he produced between those years. This refusal to exhibit can be seen as the first stage in his growing indifference to public response to his work, his alienation from current artistic trends and withdrawal into relative reclusivity. The handful of later shows were low-key affairs; his arm was twisted by wife and friends to let them take place at all, and he hated every moment. All this was in the greatest possible contrast to the decade of the 1950s in which he was widely acclaimed and exhibited almost every year at the major London galleries.[10] It is important to a fuller appreciation of some of his less immediately accessible themes and drawings to know something of his self-willed descent from that early pinnacle of fame and where it led him.

[No. 38] *Life Study*, 1967

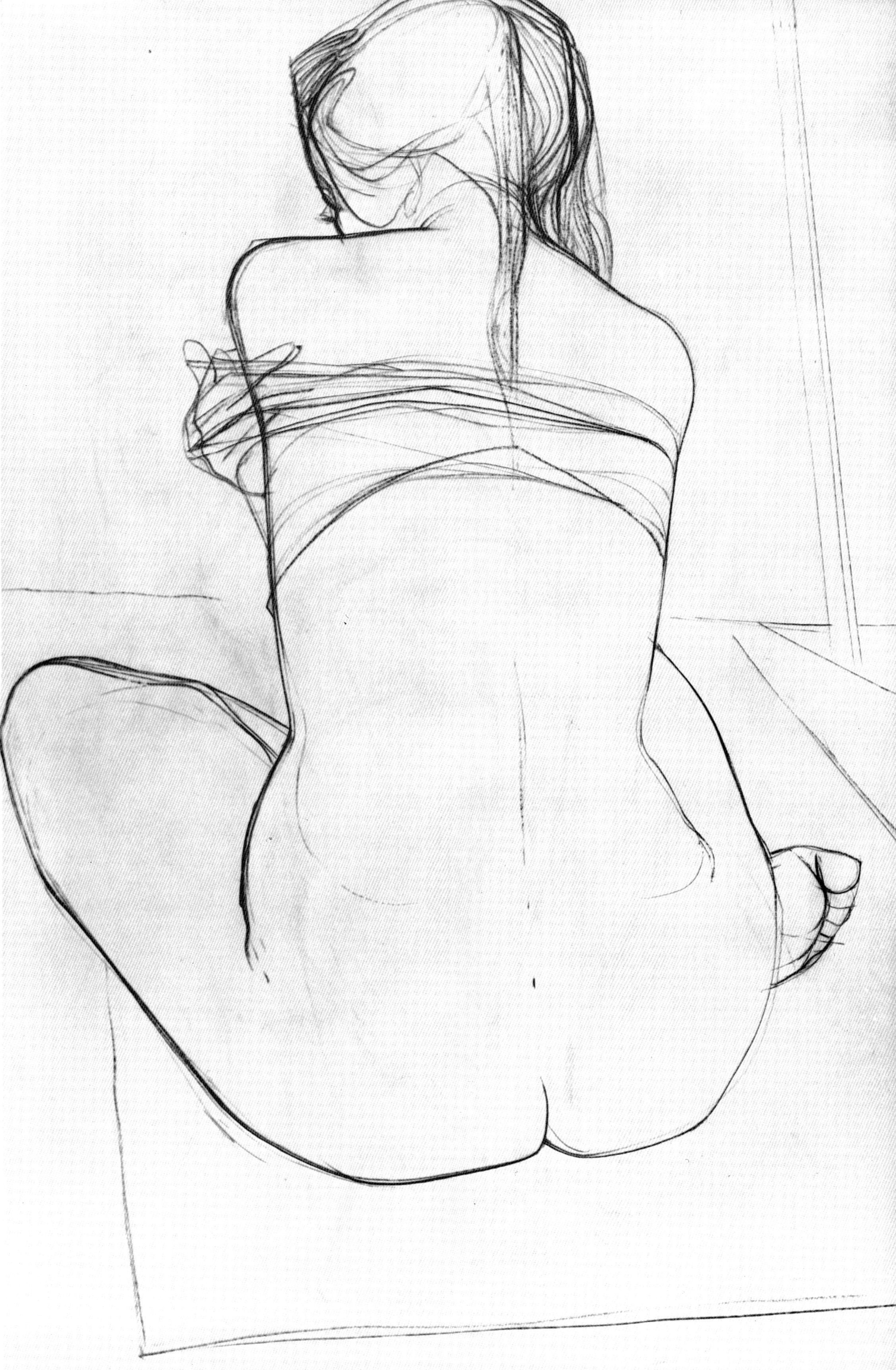

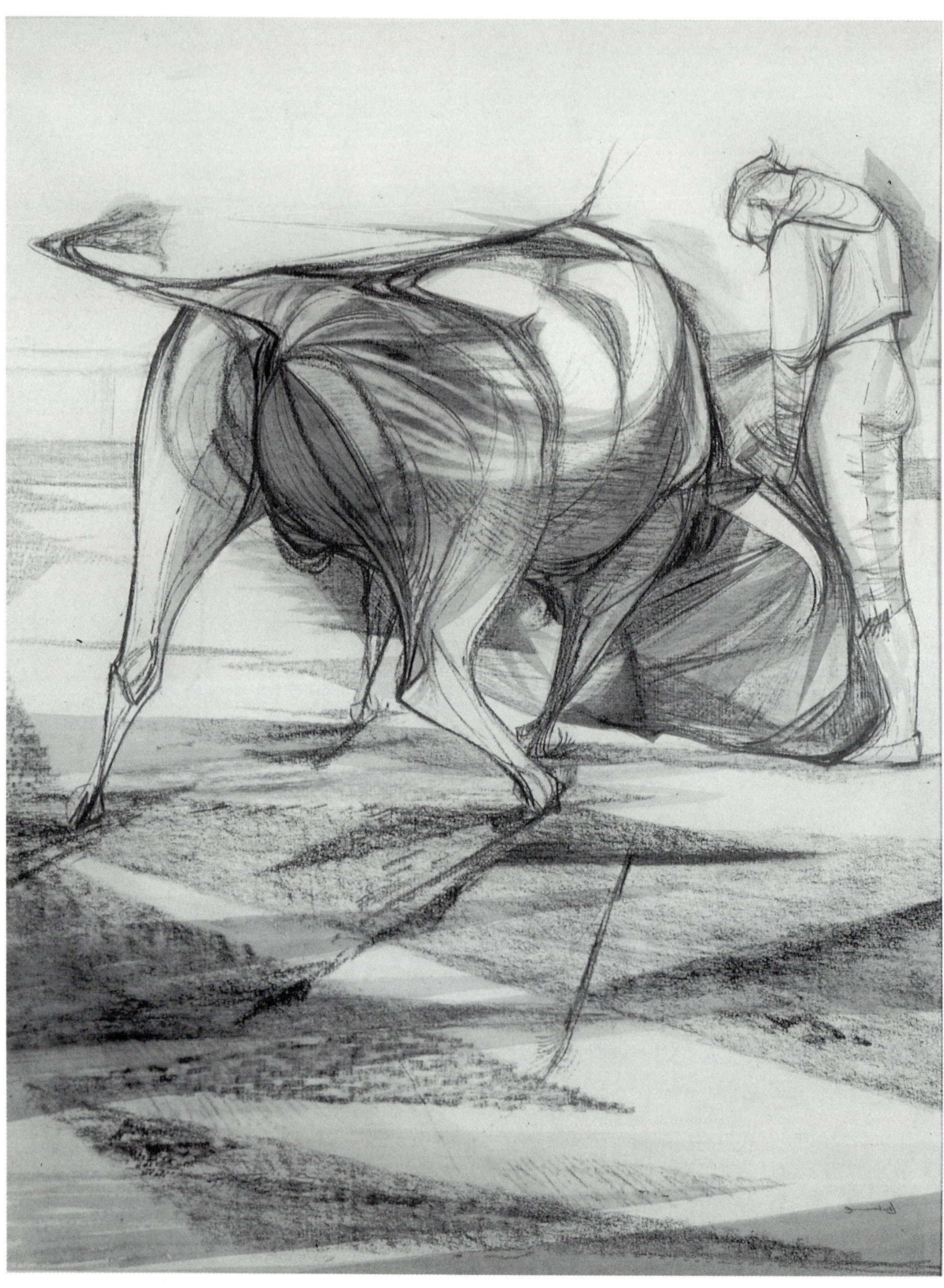

[No. 18] *The Bullfight*, c.1953

2

Lambourne's name was celebrated in the 1950s. His West End exhibitions, his drawings for the press, and the books he illustrated for the Folio Society (then at the height of its popularity) made art lovers everywhere familiar with his tough, virtuosic line drawing. I first saw original drawings in 1956 when three recent acquisitions from the 1954 Zwemmer show (nos. 6, 7 & 8) went on display at Nottingham Castle Museum. Once seen, these early drawings of bullfighters and bathers were never to be forgotten; and I have frequently heard people who saw his London shows at the time recall the experience years later–and they then usually go on to enquire what became of him: when, why and how did such a prodigious talent disappear from the map?

The critics of the national press and of the arts papers accorded rave reviews to most of the Lambourne one-man shows, and it is worth re-examining what they saw, as well as what they were looking for, in him:

> *'Line and guts, that is what you want in drawing, not all this delicate fiddling nonsense.'* [Meninsky]... Nigel Lambourne is truly a draughtsman of the twentieth century. He is a student and master of line, vigour his characteristic; like all men of his generation, time is divided not by years but in pre-war, war, and post-war periods, and for them guts was the essential thing to survival. In the aftermath this fiddling nonsense had no meaning... Few English draughtsmen are as convincing, none more economical.

That remains as true of Lambourne's work as it was when it was written in 1954, by Eric Newton for *Art News & Review*. John Russell, reviewing Lambourne's 1956 show at the Zwemmer Gallery in the *Daily Telegraph*, found a brilliant metaphor with which to encapsulate Lambourne's procedures as a draughtsman [the italics are mine]:

> In great drawing, form and line are identified. The line is not there for its own sake; nor is the form bodied forth and laid before the observer as a dog lays a bone. Form and line (in Leonardo, let us say) become one another.
>
> Lesser draughtsmen have other methods. Some hint at the forms they portray, others map them. Mr Nigel Lambourne, whose first [*sic*] show of drawings is now on view at the Zwemmer Galleries, *sets them in a high wind, throws a net round them, and pulls it tight.* His drawing has, in fact, a splendid tension, a sense of pursuit and capture very appropriate to the tousled, heavily-built women who are his subjects. Tug and thrust are here in abundance; and–a rare quality–Mr Lambourne does not cheat. There is firmness, and not merely the look of firmness, in his drawing.

The quest for verbal formulae with which to pin down and describe the interaction of line and form in Lambourne's drawings continued to hold a fascination for contemporary critics.

Describing the same 1956 show for *The Studio,* Albert Garrett takes the image of a cage – not such a cliché at the time as it has since become:

> Lambourne's forms are constructed as a cage of fine taut lines of the least number proceeding swiftly in the right direction and starting and stopping at the dictates of exactitude. The mysterious quantity, volume, is captured with economy and simplicity inside the cage. Volume, however, is only half the work that his eloquent lines have to do. There is the relation of the volume to adjoining space, adjacent forms and the two-dimensional pictorial organisation of shapes. To achieve this consummate technique he uses line in two distinct ways. With one he defines shapes and the volume's contours. This one is visual, the other moves over and across the form cartographically and is non-visual. Together they define volume and space which calls both the aesthetic and visual senses to the fore . . . He has a close affinity with the unisonant drum-tight volumes of Henry Moore, but he has evolved a style, which, although sculptural in feeling and rendering, is completely his own.

Garrett's review concluded: 'His efforts to revive the drawing as a work of art are meeting with success, and his leadership may prove strong enough to turn the tide of English graphic art.' The use of 'leadership' here is ominous, for how does a loner with no peers or followers lead? Lambourne recognised this, as he also recognised that the direction in which the pack was headed in the 1960s was definitely not for him. As a basically shy man sheltering behind a gruff exterior, he genuinely disliked media attention and perhaps feared the responsibilities and distrusted the politics of being a leader or spokesman. Barbara Lambourne is inclined to see this as the main reason for his declining to continue along the route which was undoubtedly open to him and which would have kept him in the limelight and in the good books of the dealers. His later view of dealers and pundits was scathing, and one can only surmise that some sort of dust-up, the details of which will never be known, must have occurred to cause a parting of the ways in about 1960 – whereon, leaving the dealers nothing to promote and the critics nothing to write about, Lambourne left their stage.[11]

Since the 1950s, Lambourne's name has been kept before the public, if at all, through those books which he continued to illustrate for the Folio Society. They published ten volumes with his drawings, prints or photogrammes at intervals between 1949 and 1983. I first met him as a colleague in 1962 when he came to lecture in what is now the Faculty of Graphic Design at Leicester Polytechnic. For a long time he wouldn't show me any of his current work or talk very much about it, let alone admit the thought of holding another exhibition. He had evidently been very deeply hurt at some stage, yet neither his wife nor his closest friends can to this day identify the precise build-up of emotions and circumstances which caused him to turn his back on the art world. He was stoical about the lot he had chosen and there was rarely a reference to it and never a trace of self-pity in his conversation. Years later he wrote: 'I find there is something oddly flattering to find I am "remembered" as the draughtsman of this: illustrator of that. Not without a courteously veiled surprise that I have not had a memorial show. All good black fun . . .'[12]

I must have importuned him for eighteen months or so, I suppose, until the day came when he thrust at my wife and myself a portfolio of drawings which he had retrieved from behind the bar – telling us to take them away and choose one – as he scuttled away in an

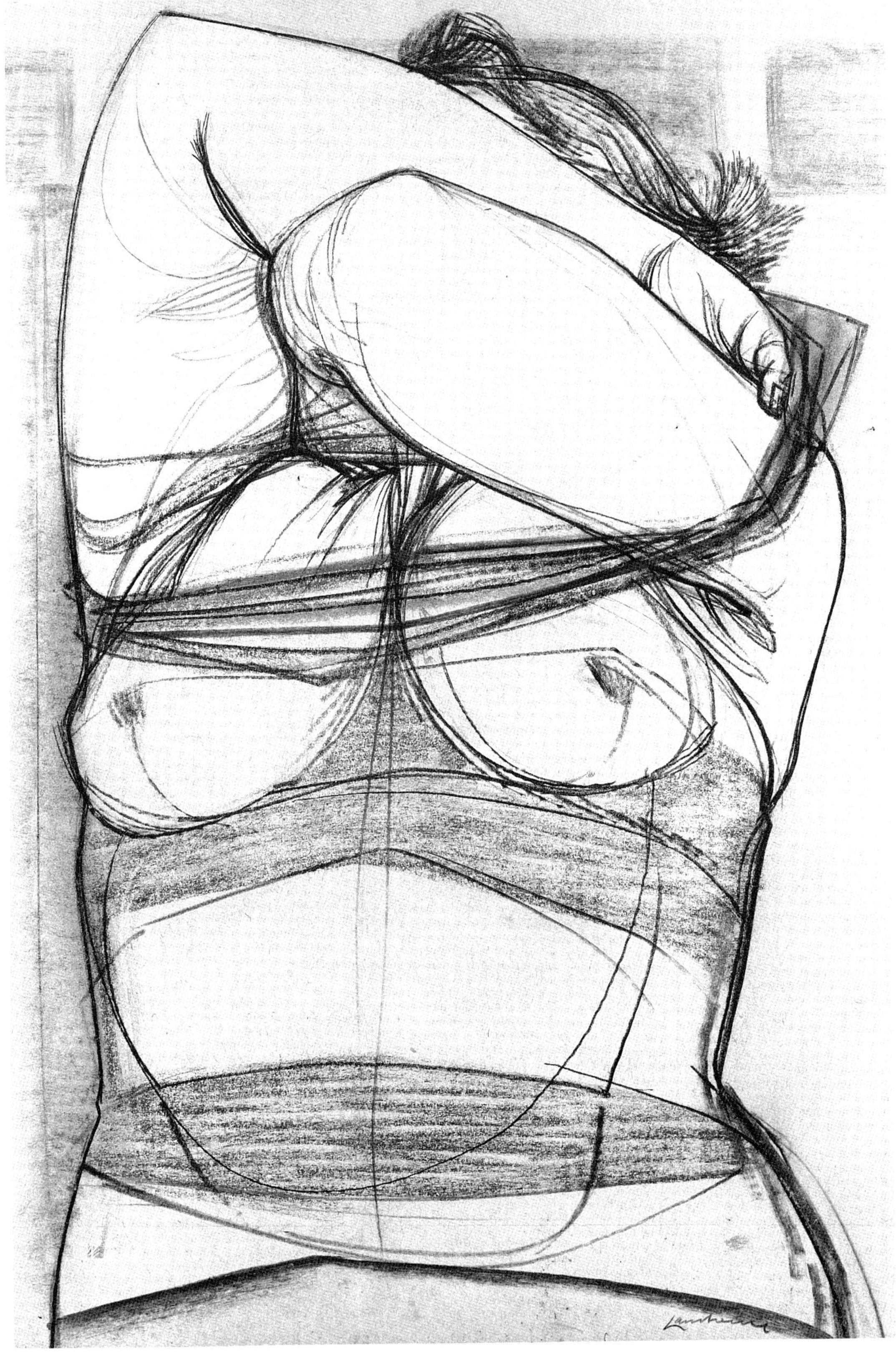

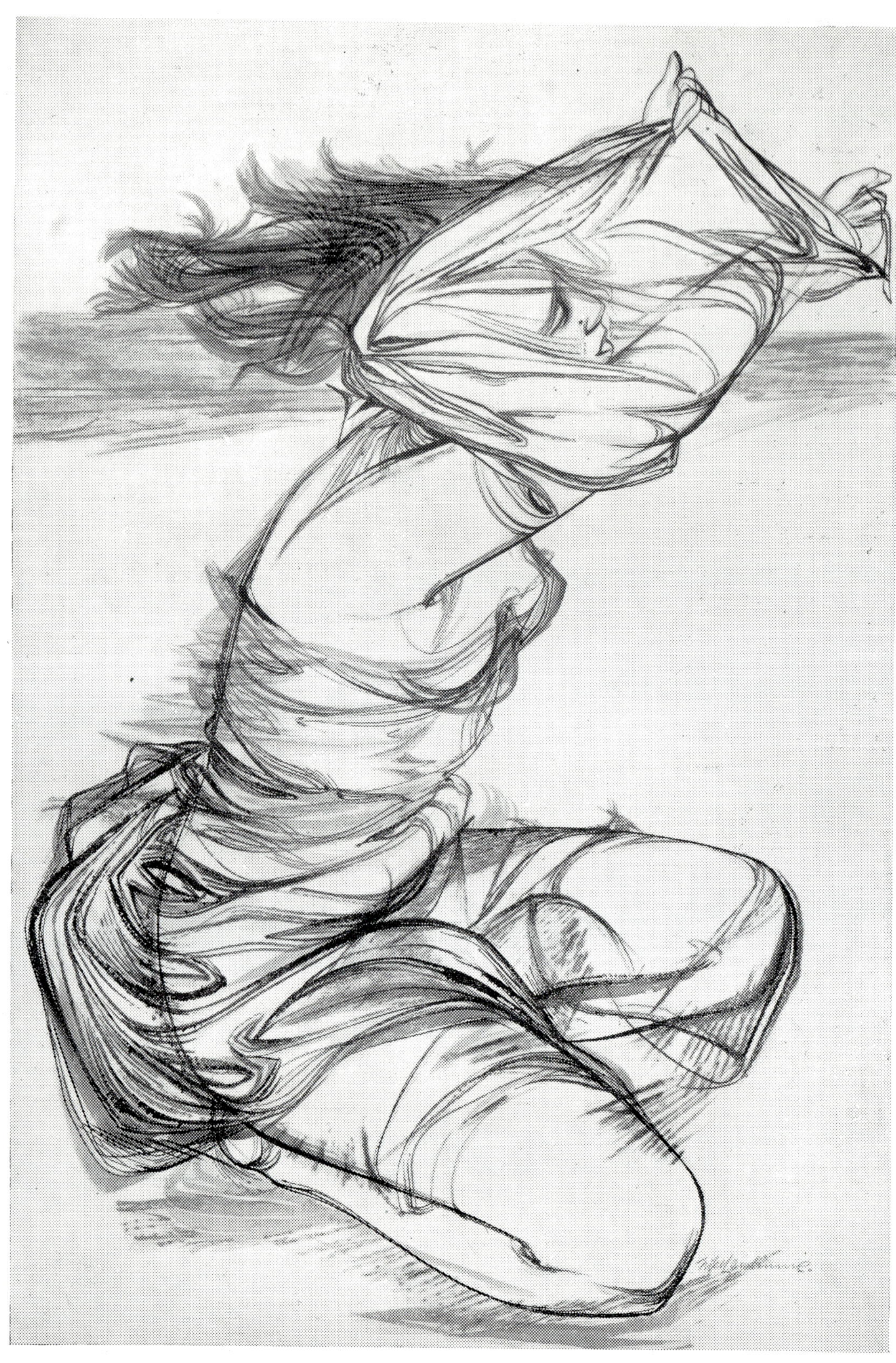

Zephyr, press drawing for Ford, 1962 [whereabouts unknown]

apparent black mood. He was probably embarrassed and at the same time fearful that we might say the wrong things; we were equally apprehensive that a slowly forming friendship could even yet collapse, as we had seen happen to others. If we were still somewhat in awe of an artist whose bark proved worse than his bite, but who was nevertheless preceded by a formidable reputation for verbally defenestrating or otherwise disposing of fools, this was nothing to the shock the contents of the folder induced. Here was great drawing and light hidden from the world.

The first two Lambourne drawings which entered our collection were the *Life Study*, 1967 (no. 38), and *Scarecrow Image from the Text of* 'Dog Years' *by Günter Grass*, 1968 (no. 40). These exemplified at the time, and still do, those two polarities in his work: drawing from life and drawing on the imagination. To varying degrees each approach was susceptible to a process of development towards the abstract; and it was during the 1960s that this dialogue with (as distinct from surrender to) abstraction is most evident in his work.

At the beginning of the 1960s James Boswell noted in the *Guardian* that 'Lambourne's imagery seems independent of fashion, cult, or trend . . .', but this proved a dangerous decade in which to try to maintain such a position in the arts. Lambourne was in fact to shift his style in the direction of greater abstraction in those years, but his way of doing so was to identify the forces and rhythms dominant in a figurative composition and reinforce them. In any case all his drawing has this innate quality of abstraction in the sense of selection and reduction, and the discovery of a play of tensions and forces that generates a composition rather than a study from life. Oswald Blakeston put it rather well: 'Often he achieves a totally abstract concept without distortion of form or making an inanimate image.'[13]

A slightly earlier generation of British artists had taken similar paths from their respective starting points in landscape and figure drawing, and so what resulted at this time for Lambourne had affinities with an established and waning language rather than subscribing to any of the kinds of abstraction which were then coming into fashion. For all its vigour his work retained an analytical quality, and he preferred to keep both romanticism and abstract expressionism at arm's length. To have tried to work in any other way than his own would have been utterly false and out of the question, and this in itself may account sufficiently for his withdrawal from the fray and refusal to exhibit. For developments in the early 1960s removed Lambourne almost overnight from his position in the vanguard of his generation to a conservative and isolated niche. Of course he understood what had happened to him and why, and yet realised that there was nothing at all that could be done about it consistent with retaining his artistic integrity. There was no way he could become an 'abstract' or a 'pop' artist.

Having said that, no artist can be entirely unaffected by the currents of the age even whilst swimming against them, and Lambourne, in common with other figurative artists, did for a time respond to the challenge of discovering where certain lines of abstract enquiry might lead. The short answer has to be that unless this process went ahead at its own pace and in accordance with his own imperatives, it merely resulted in formalism: in the mannered elaboration of rhythmic and pattern qualities latent in any figurative composition. This tendency had already expressed itself in a controlled and successful way in the great sequences of the 1950s – what Charles Keeping once called the 'mind-boggling' bullfighters and paddlers, where we almost have two drawings superimposed: an observational one and another which informs us about tensions and impacts, thrusts and strains, expending or impending movements. If the nature of these procedures can be conveyed, as a contemporary critic attempted, his later styles can be seen to evolve from this triumphant early break-through:

> Nigel Lambourne . . . has discovered the hidden lines of force that swing rhythmically round a torso or a limb, explaining not only its bulk but its muscular tensions. For this purpose he takes as his subject what could be most simply described as fat women in movement that is always purposeful but never violent and then proceeds to clothe them in a network of wonderfully fluent line that gives a new meaning to form and movement. This is a real draughtsmanly invention. There is a noble monumentality, a tense grandeur about his drawings. One is reminded of Leonardo's obsession with the dynamics of flowing water and rippling hair.[14]

Lambourne was fond of using the old showman's catch-phrase, 'Now you see it – now you don't!', which became a kind of motto for him. It describes to perfection the way in which many of his drawings dazzle the viewer, not through superfluous technical brilliance, but by the controlled use he makes of paradox and interpenetrating images. Often it is an age-old strategem that is being given a new twist – such as his use of mirrors within a composition – although other ideas are very much of his own devising. We can follow some of the best-known of these through a few of their major thematic developments and reappearances.

Shortly after the bullfighting series came studies of kite flying, and some of sailors or fishermen hauling on lines to manipulate the rigging, and the great abstract shapes of sails pressed against the sky (no. 21). In other words, these themes are chosen because they winch up yet further the tensions that were established between figure and object, between toreador and cloak, force and counter-force, in the earlier sequence. This linear experience is exhilarating for the viewer precisely because Lambourne's preoccupation is never for an instant a sculptural one, and frequently there can be no ultimate reading or resolution of the paradox which he has set up. The eye repeatedly tracks the lines of force out from and back to the heart of the composition, traversing the modelling only where this is an intended part of the linear orbit.

From this it is but a step for Lambourne to involve the viewer's eye in positing a line for itself. He can set up a trapeze situation so that the inevitability of the trajectory is anticipated by the onlooker in relation to the available data. In the unpublished illustrations for *Ulysses* (nos. 41 and 42), he even goes as far as to superimpose two protagonists' respective perceptions of the same situation within a single drawing. It may not be fanciful to suggest that the numerous albums of entertainers and strippers which flowed from him over the years correspond in broad function to Franz Liszt's *Transcendental Studies*, as the composer designated those pieces in which he pursues advanced pedagogical studies, goes on reconnaissance into no-man's land, and at the same time provisions his own repertoire as a virtuoso. This is the art of the stopwatch; the drawing there's no chance to make in real time; the pose that can't be held. Now you see it, now you don't!

[No. 12] *A Paddler*, early 1950s

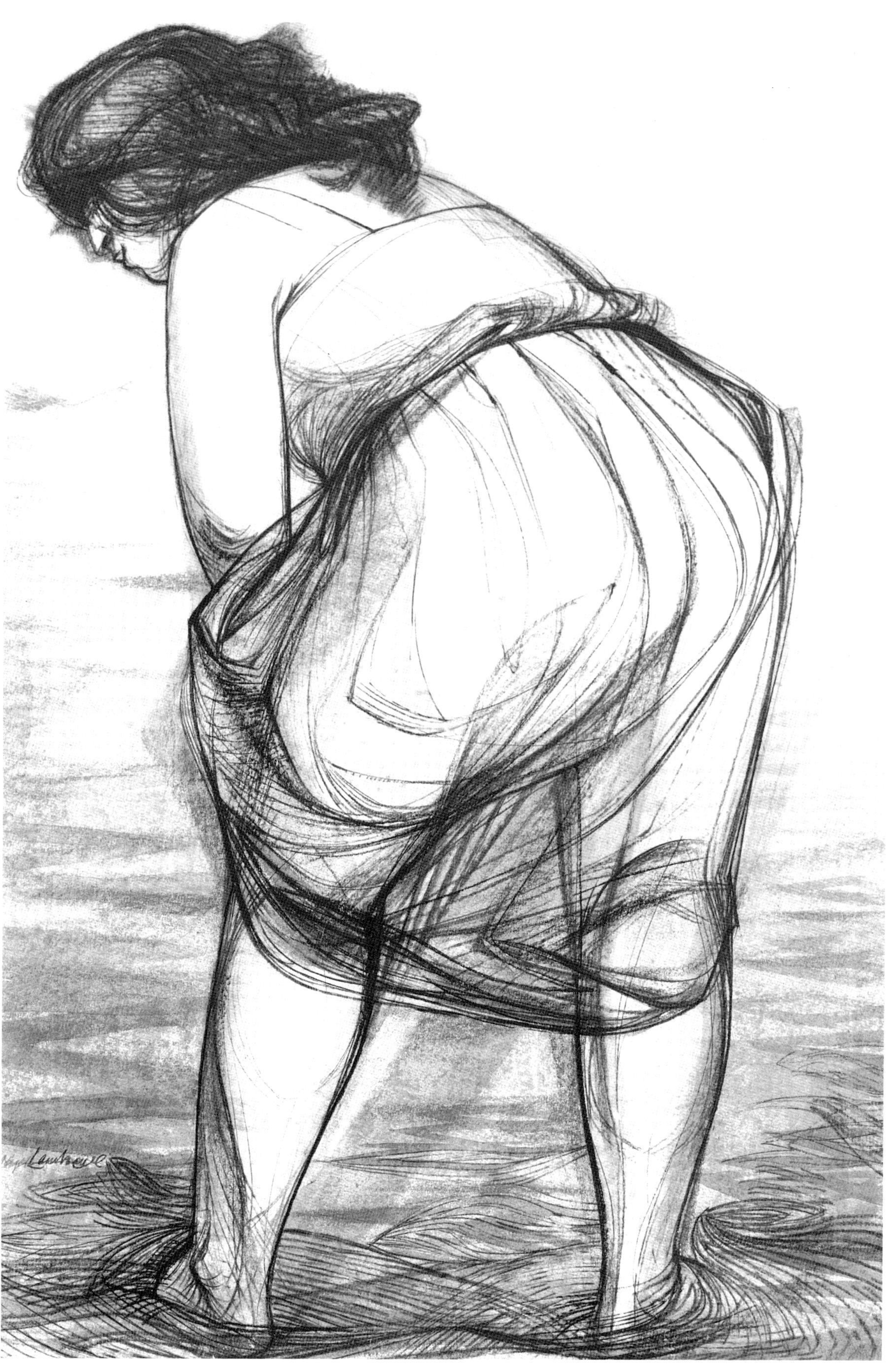

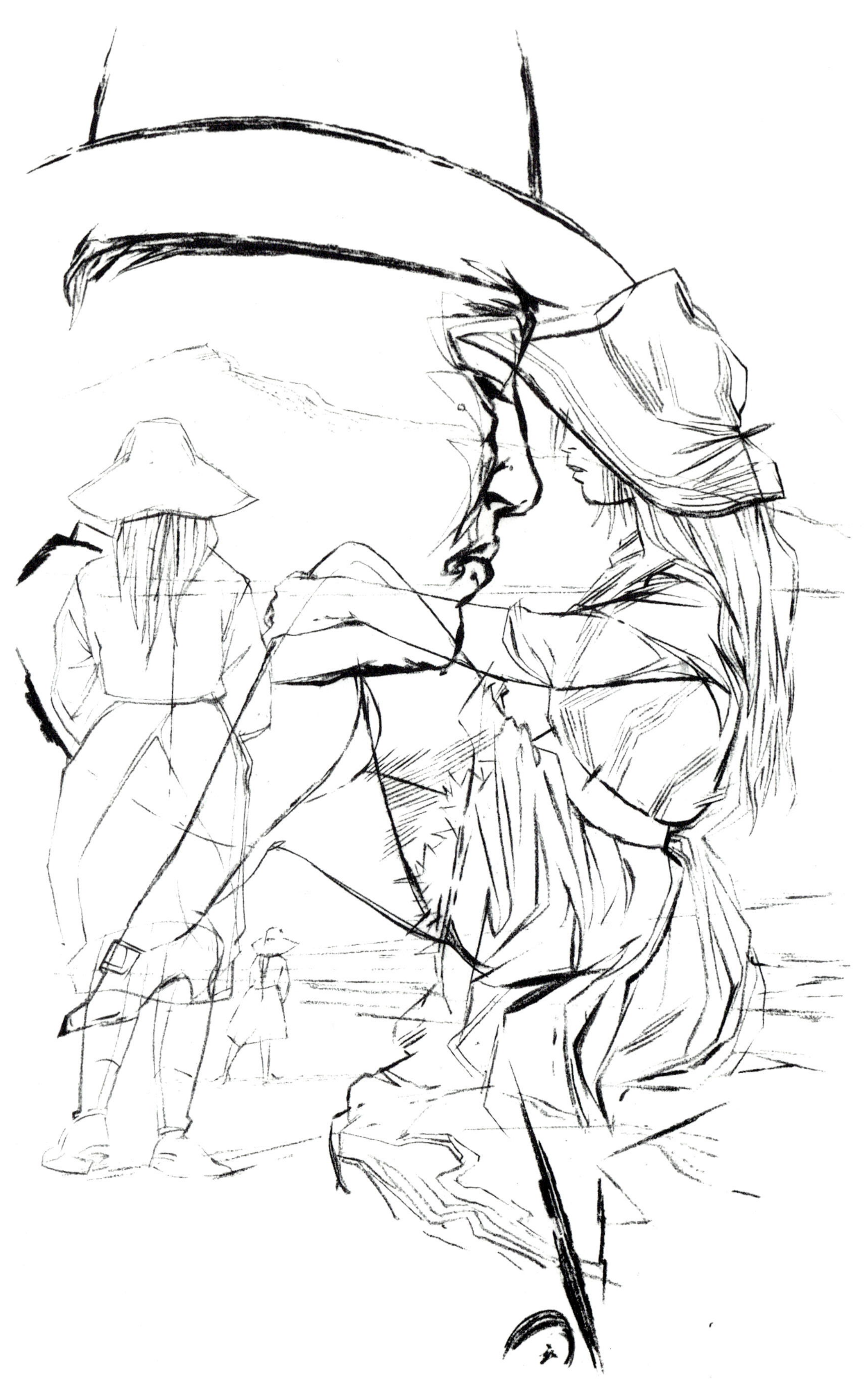

[No. 42] *Bloom, Sea-shore & Gertie*, c.1968

3

Lambourne was never a member of any school or movement; neither was he for long influenced by–nor did he work in a similar vein to–any other artist. Comparisons with more prominent contemporaries are accordingly rather pointless, and resemblances that may initially look quite striking rarely stand up to more rigorous examination.[15] And so what follows is more an attempt to recall those draughtsmen for whom Lambourne expressed his regard rather than to imply affinities or attribute influences: looking first at those he knew personally and had worked alongside, and then citing some international figures whom he had never met but whose work he nevertheless admired and studied.

Lambourne claimed to have met Sickert (1860-1942) once or twice in the pre-war years–as though the latter was doing his rounds in an art college atmosphere–but it is difficult to see how this can have been so. Certainly he revered Sickert as the bluff 'artists' artist' as much as for the link back to Whistler and through Whistler to Degas, and regretted that by however narrow a margin that line of succession had passed him by, or–to mix metaphors–had fizzled out because there was no one there to catch the ball. It is difficult to explain that for Lambourne such wishful thinking did not entail any hint of mendacity or name-dropping–it was enough that he ought to have had that opportunity and had gone on trying to make up for what might have been missed, whereas many an actual student had learned nothing. In that sense Lambourne was all his life a student of Degas–and of Shostakovitch and James Joyce for that matter. He also gave the impression that John Nash (1893-1977) may have taught him at the Royal College of Art in the years 1937-9, but it can no longer be established how penetrable was the wall between the Painting School where Nash taught, and the Engraving School in which Lambourne was enrolled. It is when Lambourne turns infrequently to landscape that his debt to both Paul and John Nash, and perhaps to the official artists of both wars in general, becomes evident. Whether rendering the levels of the Gower coastline or the Turkish interior, this terrain is depopulated and aircraft-wing grey. Military service for the duration of the war had made him attuned to the English vision of this kind of empty landscape trailing off into abstraction. Only in the studies of rock formations made in the quarries at Groby and Bethesda does Lambourne confront yet more resolutely non-figurative subject matter.

In a taped discussion, Lambourne once cited Bernard Meninsky (1891-1950) as the last of this trio of putative mentors. According to Barbara Lambourne he knew Meninsky quite well, but she thinks it unlikely that Nigel should actually have been taught by him at the Regent Street Polytechnic. Certainly some of the life drawings of both artists must rank among the finest produced this century, and it is probable that they would have got on well together. His actual tutors at the Polytechnic included Clifford Ellis and Stuart Tresilian–whom Lambourne always spoke of with affection as a remarkable teacher who had also done much to develop students' musical appreciation through extra-mural hospitality. Malcolm Osborne (1880-1963), Professor of Engraving at the RCA, taught Lambourne during both his pre- and post-war years there, but Osborne's own artistic work rarely came up for discussion and so there is little real indication of the significance Lambourne attached to his influence. But in the case of his assistant and successor, Robert Austin (1895-1973), there is I believe a link to be made in terms of discernible stylistic and technical influence.

I visited the comprehensive show of Robert Austin's work held at Leicester in 1981 in Lambourne's company, and the regard and affection he had for the man and his work became evident as he appraised each subject inch by inch. This teacher had influenced him in at least three distinct and direct ways: technically and stylistically – as in the tiny Rembrandtesque landscape etchings which Lambourne produced as apprentice work; intellectually – through the clarity and incisiveness of engraved line expected by a Royal Academician who went on to design the nation's banknotes in 1960; and in an approach to life drawing. Austin had set up his own life class as an innovation within the Engraving School, and another former student recalled his draughtsmanship in terms that could almost equally be applied to Lambourne himself:

> He was a draughtsman in the great tradition of Ingres and Degas (he would have claimed a greater affinity with the latter) and he shared their ability to make profound statements of beguiling simplicity. The thing that surprised us most however, was the size and boldness of his drawings, which were often of imperial size. These were as unlike the 'tight' drawings normally produced by engravers as could be imagined. But then he was a man overflowing with energy, who would urge us to draw as if holding a red hot needle.[16]

That other master printmaker, John Buckland-Wright, had been one of a handful of colleagues whose outlook Nigel could engage with, and his early death came as a great blow. Nigel made few friends – and fewer still as he grew older and more isolated – and when he lost them, sadly and inevitably it left its mark. In contrast to their rarity, such friendships as he kept up were lasting concerns: important for and valued by both parties, and characterised by great loyalty, forthrightness and bonhomie. Buckland-Wright's book on etching and engraving[17] contains material that grew out of their technical exchanges, and is dedicated in part to Nigel.[18]

It has been mentioned in passing that for a time Buckland-Wright, Lambourne and Clifford Hall formed an artistic trio, meeting regularly at the latter's studio (where they were sometimes joined by Charles Lambert). Nigel was of a slightly younger generation, but it must have been natural for him to gravitate towards the company of like-minded artists with greater technical experience in some matters. Clifford Hall (until his death in 1973) and his second wife Ann remained closer to Nigel perhaps than any other artists. Although Clifford was primarily a painter, he apprehended Nigel's stature as a draughtsman, as can be seen from the slightly irascible notes he made after his two visits to the 1971 show:

> What a show! It should have been given the right presentation. As it is his drawings are in a "gallery" cluttered with appalling Art Nouveau bric-à-brac, glass cabinets of

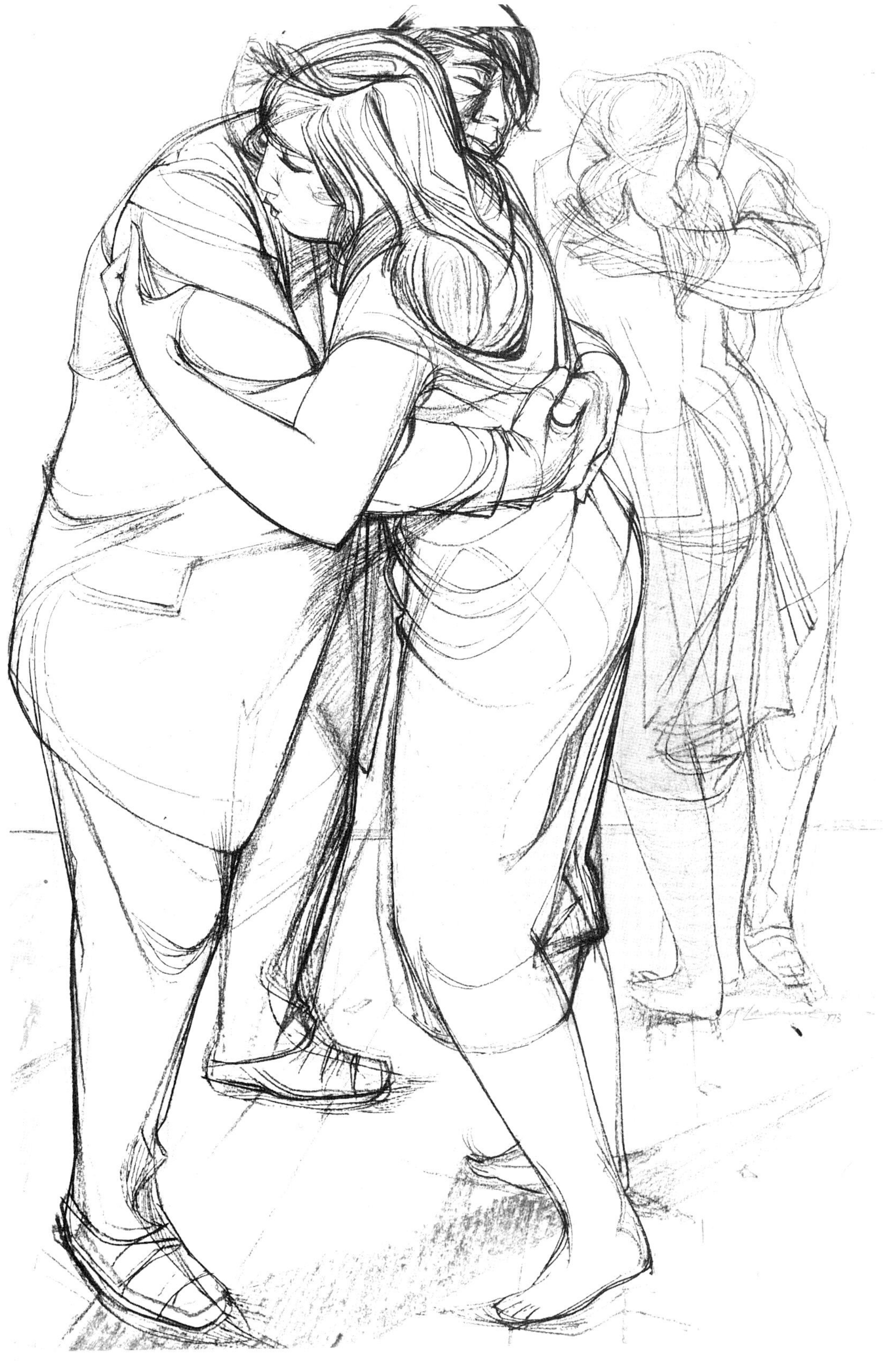

[No. 25] *Marathon Dancers*, 1950s

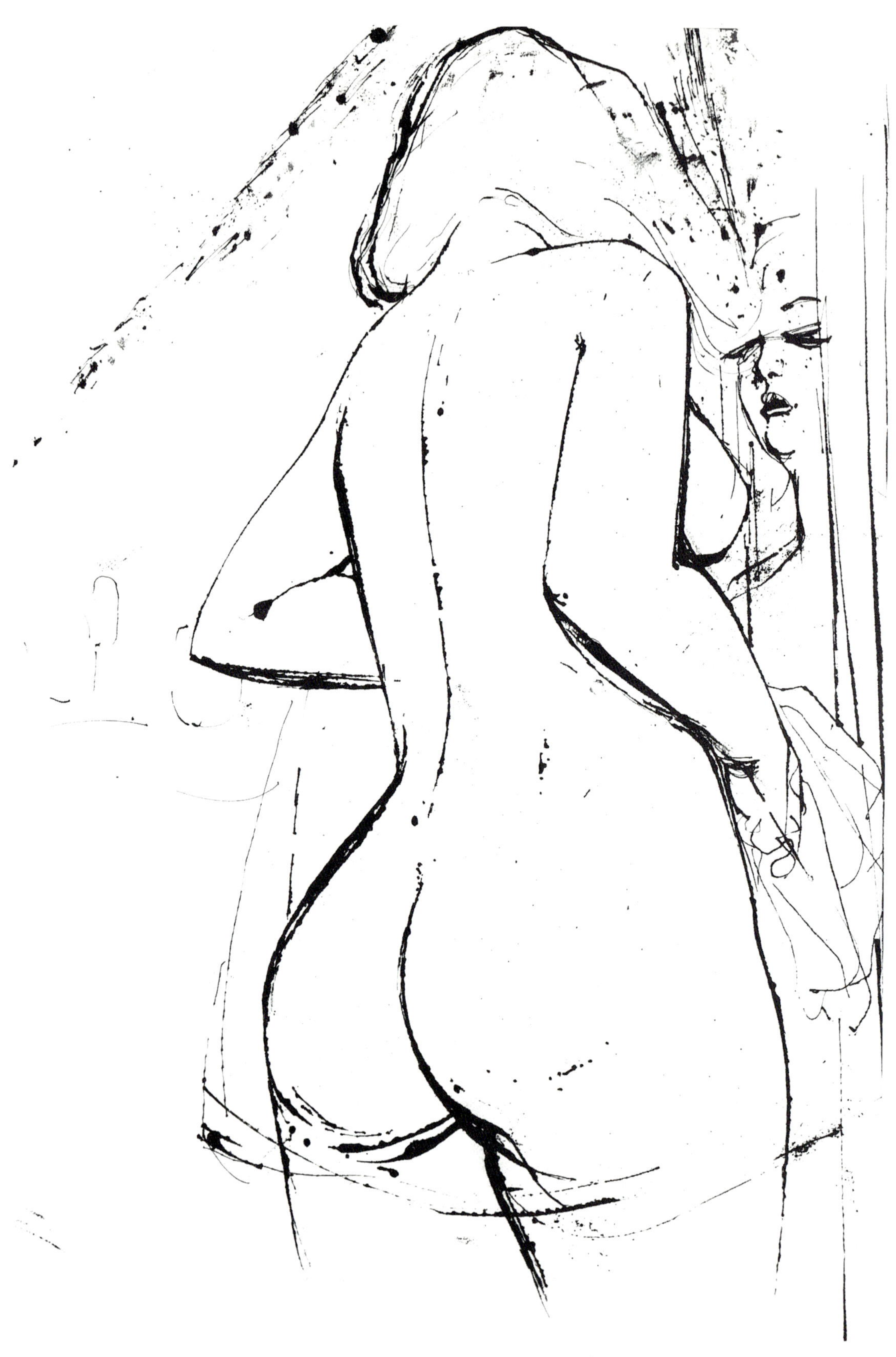

[No. 57] *Strip Entertainer*, 1974 or earlier

jewellery, bits of china – even a funny cat! It is infuriating, and fine as the drawings are this kind of setting does not help.

'The Geriatric (i)' is a masterpiece, terrifying and true. I find the nudes, strippers, lovers, curiously lacking in sensuality. They go far beyond this, having for me, the frightening and impersonal yet compelling quality of symbols: and always the sheer fascination of the drawing is not short of miraculous. So these lovers and couples embracing are not at all erotic – compared with the Indian sculptures or the Picasso series . . .

. . . Went to N's exhibition for 2nd time this P.M. and was glad to see there had been some sales. In spite of the bric-à-brac with which the drawings are surrounded their impact remains terrific . . . Words fail when one compares him with the mostly pointless experiments and so-called 'happenings' that are taken seriously at present; and particularly by the Arts Council, these posturings by young men, often, predictably American, who can neither draw nor paint: never could and never will . . .[19]

If Lambourne's call to arms on behalf of drawing had gone largely unheeded, his involvement with book illustration and the increasing realignment of his work to exploring themes drawn from world literature was to break new and fruitful ground. In turning from being an artist-printmaker towards illustration for similar reasons, his career was closely paralleled by that of his one-time pupil and near-contemporary Charles Keeping (1924-1988).[20] Each held the other's work in the regard reserved for equals by those at the pinnacle of their profession. This emerges generously from a letter Lambourne wrote in connection with an illustrated article on Keeping I had sent for his opinion:

They are (all the drawings of any state) the most *complete* definition of draughtsmanship I can think of. This, without reference to their function, – as 'illustration' – each with a life of its own. As I go back over them, there is not *one* I would not dearly love to say (then and now) – that, 'I did this or that, so there it is'. End of quote. Anyway, I most surely am cut down to size. It's never enough to look back on any one piece of work and consider its merit. The 'one off'. Christ knows I've done a *few*! But brother Charles does it one after another and that is a fair definition of what being a great draughtsman means, rather than being merely talented. Maybe, I'll now have a stab at the bassoon. I've always loved the instrument and there at least I would not have the same kind of competition? Of course I don't know. With the Ch. K. fluency *he* could probably belt out Vivaldi before I mastered a key change.[21]

He was devastated at the news of the younger man's death just over six months before his own. I have linked these two artists because together in post-war Britain they carried a quality of drawing that properly begins in the academic life-class (and may so easily end there) far beyond, into a creative and progressive engagement with literature and other themes of universal significance. Moreover they accomplished this at a time when that tradition was disregarded and had fallen into desuetude in the art colleges. Life classes were discontinued at the Royal College of Art itself from the early 1960s until the appointment of Bryan Neale as

Professor of Drawing in 1991.[22] As the climate changes and conceptual art palls, the work of such inspired draughtsmen as Lambourne and Keeping will be seen afresh by a new generation, and I believe there is ample evidence that this is beginning to happen.

Connoisseurs of drawing will place Lambourne in a different perspective than general students of British art in the twentieth century in any case. Schools, '-isms' and allegiances are not so important in this context, and the concept of progress is seen for the delusion it is. Many will be inclined to rank him highly indeed alongside the finest draughtsmen of other ages and of other nations and to feel confident that his position in that company is secure.

During the Leicester years, when not to be found at Yates' Wine Lodge at lunchtime, Nigel would be sure to be in the Leicester Polytechnic Library. His favourite stations were by the international art journals or the books just received, where he stood or paced about, turning pages furiously and audibly. Little of substance can have escaped this early warning system, which scanned right across the arts and was international in coverage for the periods that concerned him. These were from early baroque to the enlightenment, and again from the beginning of the twentieth century to the avant-garde. The old masters and the nineteenth century he knew well from student days, and most of what he needed was already on his own shelves. The secondhand bookshops, none more so than those of the West Country and the Welsh border towns, especially Hay-on-Wye – from which the Lambournes' library had in large part been assembled – continued to exert a fascination for them long after there were no more real finds to be made.

Whenever there was a significant development on the international scene, as when an artist or group hitherto unknown outside delimited geographical confines achieved a breakthrough, Lambourne knew about it and had studied the work. The catalogue of artists whose work Nigel first made known to others in this way is considerable, but to instance just three in order of discovery: Georg Gross, Egon Schiele, Hans Bellmer. Among other book illustrators, he had always got on well with Michael Ayrton, Edward Bawden and Paul Hogarth, and had a strong admiration for the engraved work of Garrick Palmer and practically everything he had seen by the American artist Leonard Baskin.

He would never miss an exhibition which he thought might prove interesting if he could afford a visit, and although he didn't make any special effort to attend live concerts in the years I knew him, his holiday postcards from France make clear that he liked to catch up with public performances by 'authentic' baroque ensembles whose work he knew from record. On the whole he preferred recorded music and the chance it gave for repeated hearings. Similarly he would usually choose to find his way into a play from a script rather than from a stage performance. He was lastingly grateful to anyone going on an overseas trip who would take the trouble to track down an obscure text or tape for him, and generally kept himself culturally and intellectually as well informed in darkest Leicestershire as he might have done in the heart of London, Paris or Milan.

Club Entertainer, 1977 [whereabouts unknown]

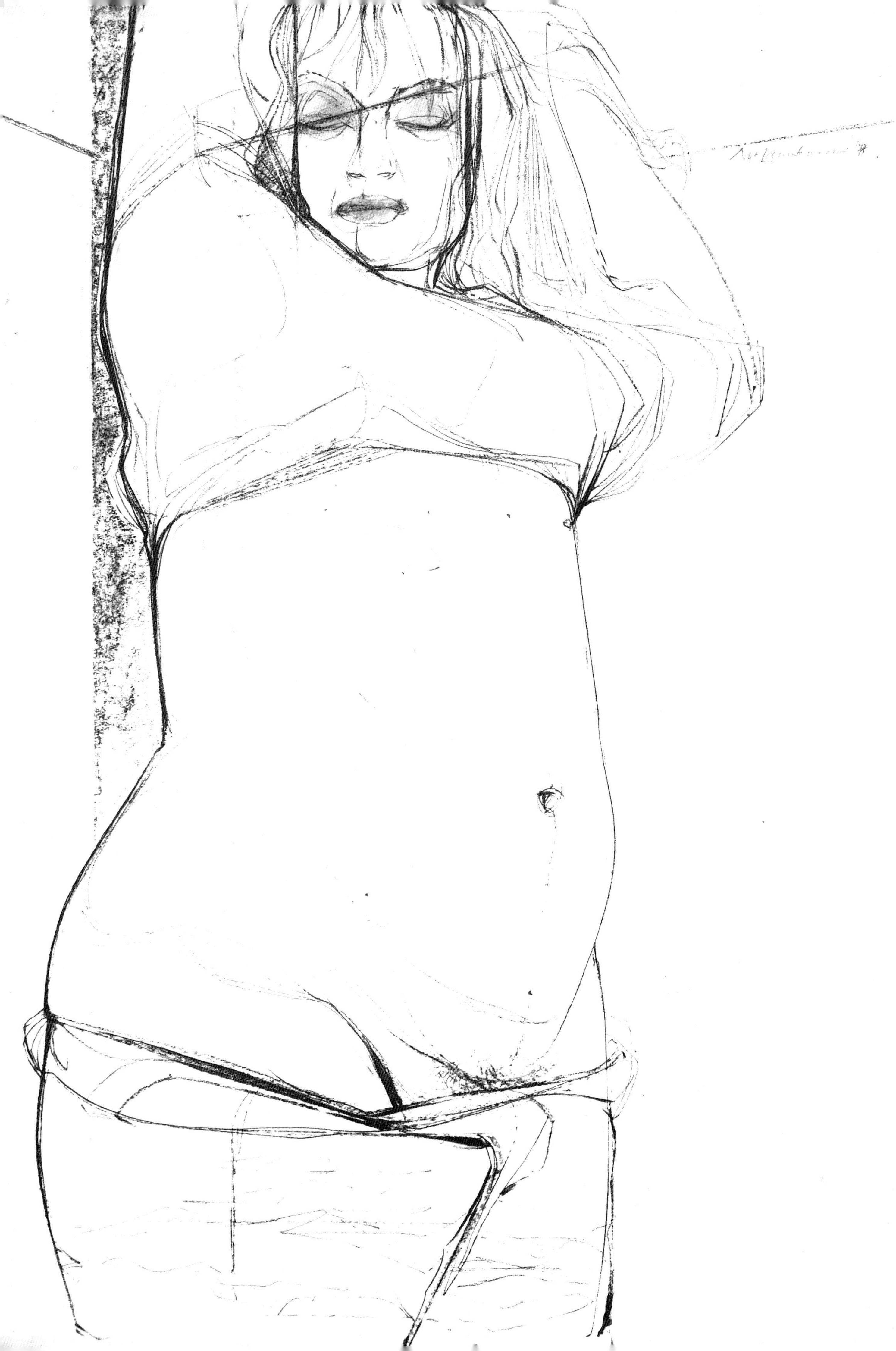

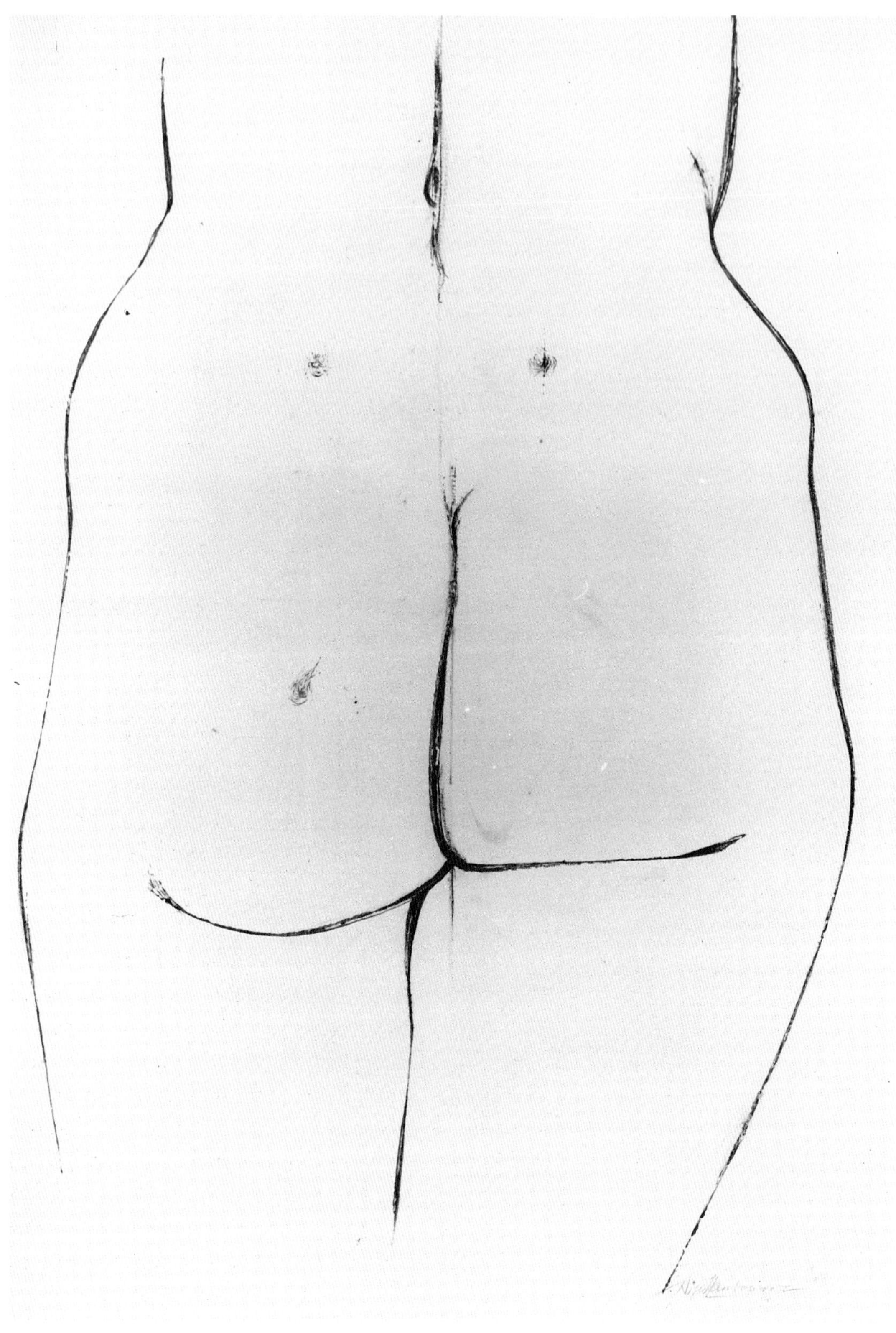

[No. 75] *Diagram of a Torso, Maybe?*, 1988

4

After the Lambournes' move to Somerset in 1984, Nigel's attic room at Oakhill was too tiny to serve as a studio. A small desk and window ledge housed a half-imperial board and a shaving mirror for self-portraiture and little else. Two or three decrepit portfolios beneath the bed contained what he had kept of his life's work. No wonder that in these spartan conditions he began to lose the will to draw in his final years – or perhaps these circumstances reflected that such a withdrawal had already taken place? Barbara Lambourne is quite sure that he made precious few if any drawings at Oakhill, and yet he generally spoke and wrote as though nothing had changed, sending the odd drawing as usual and letting it be assumed to be recent. Indeed one drawing, *Diagram of a Torso, Maybe?* (no. 75), is dated 1988, and arrived in September of that year with one of his last letters, in which he gives the impression that he is still working:

> Amigos – Before another departure into some maelstrom maybe – ? I wanted you to have another version of a torso: a 'diagram' of a torso maybe. I am much happier with it than any versions you may have?
>
> It is not a little sick that so many of those I knew are 'off the hook' and the rest are simply art-ing on, because it is a very nervous tic and obviously terminal/incurable. Mine is private: and I certainly do/am 'art-ing', but O so quietly. It was Nicholas Hilliard the Elizabethan miniaturist who said "... it is withal, secret yet cleanly, that few may know what one doeth ..." Hooray![23]

Despite this avowal, it is impossible to avoid the impression that he had largely put his artistic affairs in order during these final months, leaving a minimal kit within reach to record the odd footnote or amendment as it arose. His mind still appeared to be busied with creative matters, however, and he took to writing long and frequent letters full of projects and dreams. Earlier and, one suspects, often in his cups, he had sent off sporadic letters in this vein – interspersed with his regular postcards from the Midi charting the vintage – but this rather one-sided correspondence now became a habit taking the place of the gatherings which would have been more frequent had we sensed how little time was left to him. Letters were also sent in amends for his refusal to come to the telephone under any circumstances – even complicated two-way traffic had to be conducted via Barbara as Nigel cursed and growled in the background. One of the letters he sent after the second visit to France in 1988 mentions a book illustration project, which he doubtless wrestled with mentally, although no trace survives on paper:

> Of not dis-un-connected matters, I am back into Alfred Döblin's *Berlin Alexanderplatz* (1929 and all that) and realising more than ever how valuable it was to Grass (*The Tin Drum*?) All the efforts the late Brian Rawson made on my behalf at Folio came to not

> a whimper as regards this terrific book. It is one of the few remaining efforts in so-called 'book illustration' I would rush into. But now I shall never have the right chance. Most of all, it might just have helped my incurable (terminal?) disease of the self-quotation. Unquote. Possibly . . .

His voracious reading had continued through the quasi-hibernation of the previous winter of 1987-8, as for so many years past:

> The Shostakovich encl. [*Testimony*, as related to Solomon Volkov] was the blackest thing I've read since, maybe Genet; or especially since Céline (*Journey to the End of the Night*) – and there is a lot in common with the *latter.* Maybe tho' Shostakovich was marginally *less* misanthropic than Céline; but it's a very damn near thing. Of course I enjoy them both. (They both cheer me along in an 'effing English febr: sleeting and freezing and howling for the last 48 hours.)[24]

The *Angst* which weighed such artists down reached out to correspondingly dark regions in his own make-up. Shostakovich's dread of death he shared with like intensity, although it now found little expression through drawing. But he was stoical and considerate to his friends, and, had he received any intimation of serious illness, he would never have admitted it. Throughout that winter, Barbara and he made plans for their forthcoming expedition to Turkey:

> For the so-called project of Turkeii – (after some twenty years since) – is one of doubt, dread and fascination all at the same time. A hairy drive to Venice, four days on to Izmir and then a 700 mile drag across Anatolia – one has to be really bent. At best, I could get material once more, for the lonely & deserted scrub dotted with crude memorial slabs of long deceased Ottoman landlords. I have a few records from a second trip. Tramping over the dusty mounds, careful of the giant tortoises and clouds of grasshoppers to some forlorn sandstone slab leaning into the no-where. Not to mention the heat-blaze from a white sky. Bloody bent in fact. We should have 'learned' but of course not: we sweat in whatever shade a few battered olive trees offer and think of the Alpes M., by Grasse or Valbonne or – ? and wonder why we are not *there.* Probably, one reason is that the A.M. is too cosy, too easily reached and too simply a gorgeous place to rot in before we go into the final goodnight oven, that's about it.[25]

The long trip was a huge success, and, returning to England in Barbara's words 'just to do the laundry', after a brief phone call they headed straight back for St Rémy-en-Provence.

Nigel always drove his Volkswagen camper with as sure a line as a Conté crayon. Both their houses had entries that defied vehicular access and might have been chosen for that feature, for he unerringly swung out of the paved courtyard into the lane at Oakhill in the only viable single movement – with an inch at best to spare between the stone pillars. And when it was our turn to leave, he invariably stood in the road and did his impersonation of a traffic flic, dragging hard on a Gauloise and signing-off with a baroque gesture or worse. He died suddenly at home in the early hours of Monday 12 December 1988; but that is how we shall remember him.

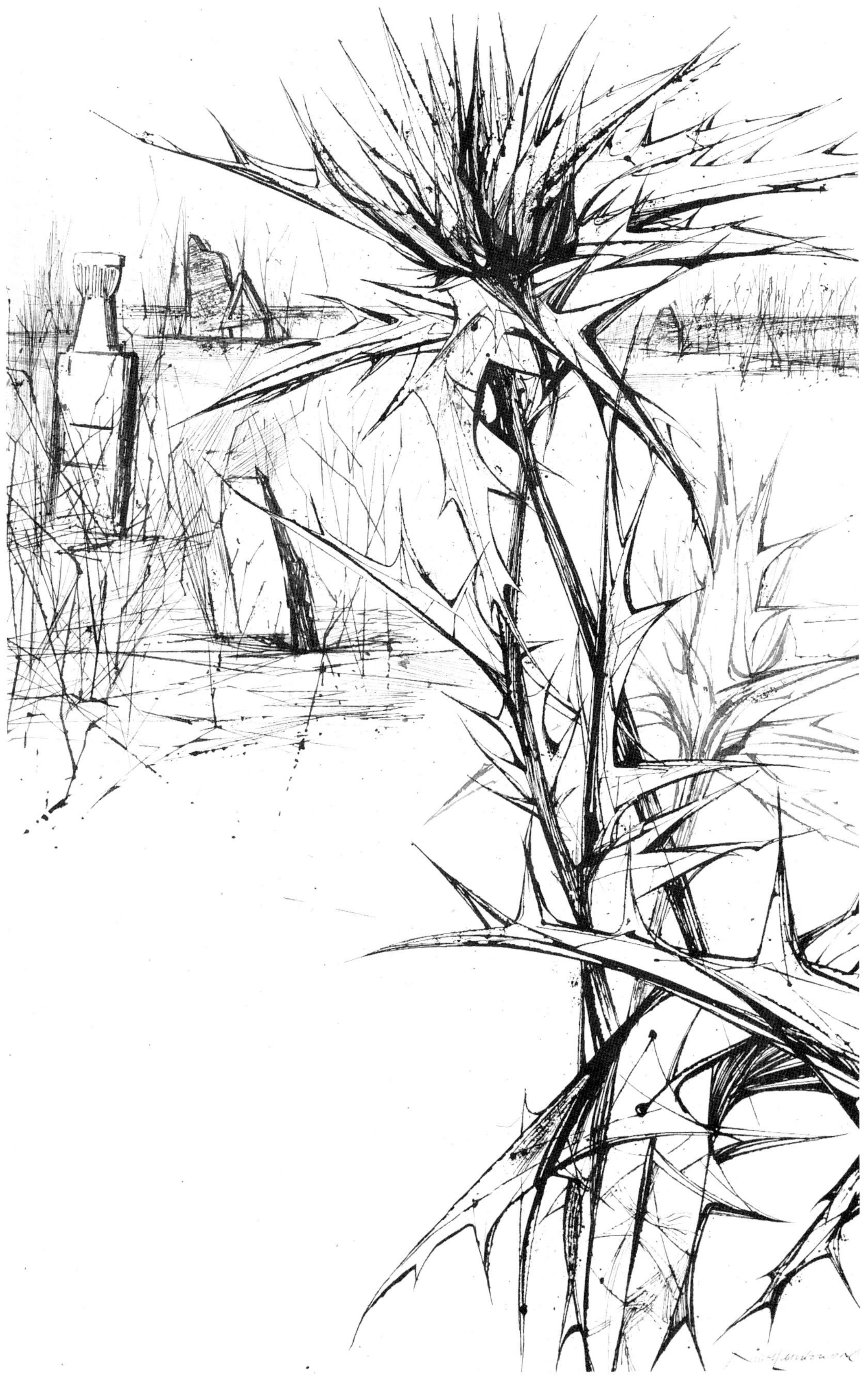

[No. 60] *Turkish Cemetery (ii)*, c.1976

Notes

1. *Renoir: paintings, drawings, lithographs and etchings,* selected and introduced by Nigel Lambourne (The Folio Society, 1965), introduction to drawings, i.
2. Barbara Lambourne: 'Nigel Lambourne', *Folio* magazine (April-June 1964), 4-7.
3. Nigel Lambourne: 'Drawing for the love of it', *The Artist* (1969), 5-6, 34-5, 54-5.
4. Lambourne's work as a book illustrator is considered in the present author's studies: 'Nigel Lambourne', *The Private Library* (3rd series, vol 5, no 1, Spring 1982), 2-24; *The Telling Line* (Julia MacRae Books, 1989), 106-25; 'Der Illustrator Nigel Lambourne' (Memmingen, *Illustration* 63, *Zeitschrift für Buchillustration,* vol 28, no 2, August 1991), 43-7.
5. 'A first draft in very soft charcoal was run over the entire contour of the squat, square, sitting shape at about half the life size scale, since the drawing was made at little more than average arm's length from the subject. At a second investigation of the spidery, broad (and inaccurate) map of the shape on the paper, another firmer series of correcting impressions were drawn *down* from each side of the shoulders, over the hips and finally meeting round the base – the buttocks. These were more rhythmical lines, but still fluid enough to allow the give and push of an infinite amount of readjustment *inside* the whole. At this point a revision of all the tentative placing, the division of each armpit to the shoulder slope, the exact balance from side to side of the elbow joints, was made in relation, once again, to the *whole.* And not least, the head was set more firmly and positively in relation to the buttocks. Thus, making a sequence of the process of adjusting from side to side and top to bottom, check and cross-check, believing, as always, that once the external shapes are true to one's image of them, the internal shapes have little option but to fall into similar truth. It is because most of us spend our whole lives looking at *little facets* of the whole that we find it so difficult to grasp the essence of the whole as one thing at our first impression.

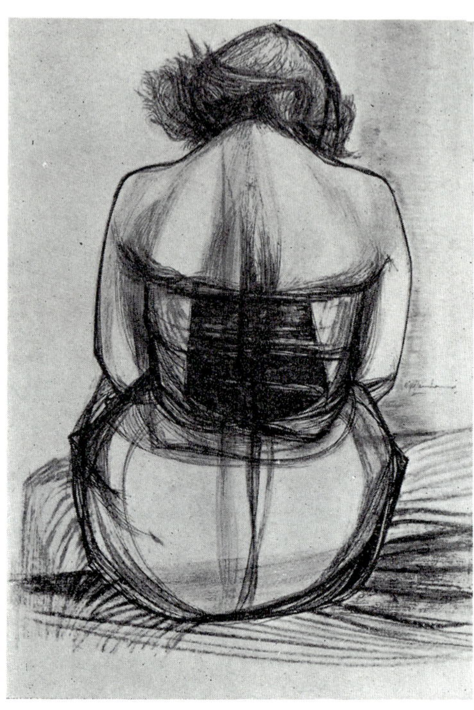

The Corset, c.1959 [whereabouts unknown]

A hard chalk, a Conté No. 2, was used from this stage onwards in all the 'firming up' and delineation of the pressing, binding lines of the corset from the inside to the outside of the torso . . . Little more was drawn from the subject herself, instead notes of such details as the number of major folds in the tension and slackness of the skirt and the mechanics of the corset itself were made. These were then transcribed and selected for use in the final stages not of elaboration, but of reassessment and drawing together of the rhythm of arms to back and skirt tensions, to the simple, suave rolling of the shoulders.

In my view, to have attempted such a study entirely from life would have meant seeing too much: seeing flesh without body shape, taut folds without the big sense of the skirt itself, and thus bearing out my belief that, to complete a picture (of any appreciable size) from Nature is tempting disaster.

In this instance (as with others cited

previously) the most logical approach was, first, through the senses; the impact of the whole impression was noted down and then a careful selection and rejection of causes towards the total effect. Not *all* the causes, because they are infinite and are there in profusion in the living subject, but much rather aim towards the distillation of the sum of the whole.' Nigel Lambourne: 'Drawing for the love of it', *The Artist* (1969), 54-5.

6. 'Nigel came at 5.30 & we drew from 6-8. What a fine fellow he is & what a good artist, one of the real ones & there are so few.' Clifford Hall: journal entry (23 February 1952).
7. Nigel Lambourne: undated letter to author (Oakhill, c.1986).
8. Nigel Lambourne: undated letter to author (Oakhill, 1984/5).
9. Nigel Lambourne: letter to author (Oakhill, 21 March 1987).
10. In his recent history (*More than a Bookshop: Zwemmer's and art in the 20th century*, Philip Wilson, 1991), 231, Nigel Vaux Halliday observes that: 'Lambourne, according to the reviewer in *Studio*, dominated the [group exhibition of 1954] with five drawings of female figures.' He goes on to make the points that these drawings reproduced very well in the press, and that all three subsequent Zwemmer one-man shows were widely and appreciatively reviewed.
11. 'Lambourne has very strong views about the contemporary art world and the relationship of his fellow artists and himself to it. One of his quarrels with certain art dealers is the practice of directing an artist to produce enough canvases for an exhibition once every six months. In this way, he says, "the artist is being made into a human trend, he embodies a style, he's made to be a pace-maker. When the trend passes away the dealer will leave the artist squeezed out like a lemon. For myself I don't think I could do it, and I never work to produce an exhibition because it is merely bowing to high-pressure salesmanship." ' Interviewed for the *Kensington Post & Advertiser*, 1965.
12. Nigel Lambourne: letter to author (Enderby, 9 October 1979).
13. Oswald Blakeston: commenting on the 1959 Wilton Gallery exhibition for the *Architectural Review*.
14. Eric Newton: writing in *Time and Tide*, 9 October 1954.
15. A parallel with Ayrton has been suggested, for example, and one can readily see two draughtsmen of outstanding intellect deriving archetypal themes from literary or mythical sources, but as to the manner of their drawing there is no resemblance, but rather an antithesis between Ayrton's sculptural vision and Lambourne's faith in the validity of two-dimensional cartography.
16. *Robert Austin* 1895-1973: *an exhibition of etchings, engravings, drawings and watercolours* (Leicestershire Museums & Art Gallery, 1981), viii.
17. John Buckland-Wright: *Etching and Engraving: techniques and the modern trend* (The Studio Publications, 1953). For Lambourne, *see* 99, *109*, 128, 134-5, 139, *142-3*.
18. 'And of course Nigel had secretly hoped for the Print School job at the Slade [this went to Anthony Gross], especially after his close connection with John and the book. He should have had the chance to run a print department; he loved the medium and its various combinations and possibilities – or at least had his own press.' Barbara Lambourne: letter (9 August 1991).
19. Clifford Hall: journal entries (1 and 10 October 1971).
20. Douglas Martin: *Charles Keeping: an illustrator's life and work*, forthcoming 1992 from Julia MacRae Books. Earlier essays have appeared in *The Telling Line* (Julia MacRae Books, 1989), 36-59; and 'Der Illustrator Charles Keeping' (Memmingen, *Illustration 63, Zeitschrift für Buchillustration*, vol 27, no 2, August 1990), 55-9.
21. Nigel Lambourne: undated letter to author (Oakhill, Autumn 1987).
22. See Jonathan Glancey: 'Students are finally coming back to life', *The Independent* (4 July 1991).
23. Nigel Lambourne: undated letter to author (Oakhill, Spring 1988).
24. Nigel Lambourne: undated letter to author (Oakhill, September 1988).
25. Nigel Lambourne: letter to author (Oakhill, 2 February 1988).

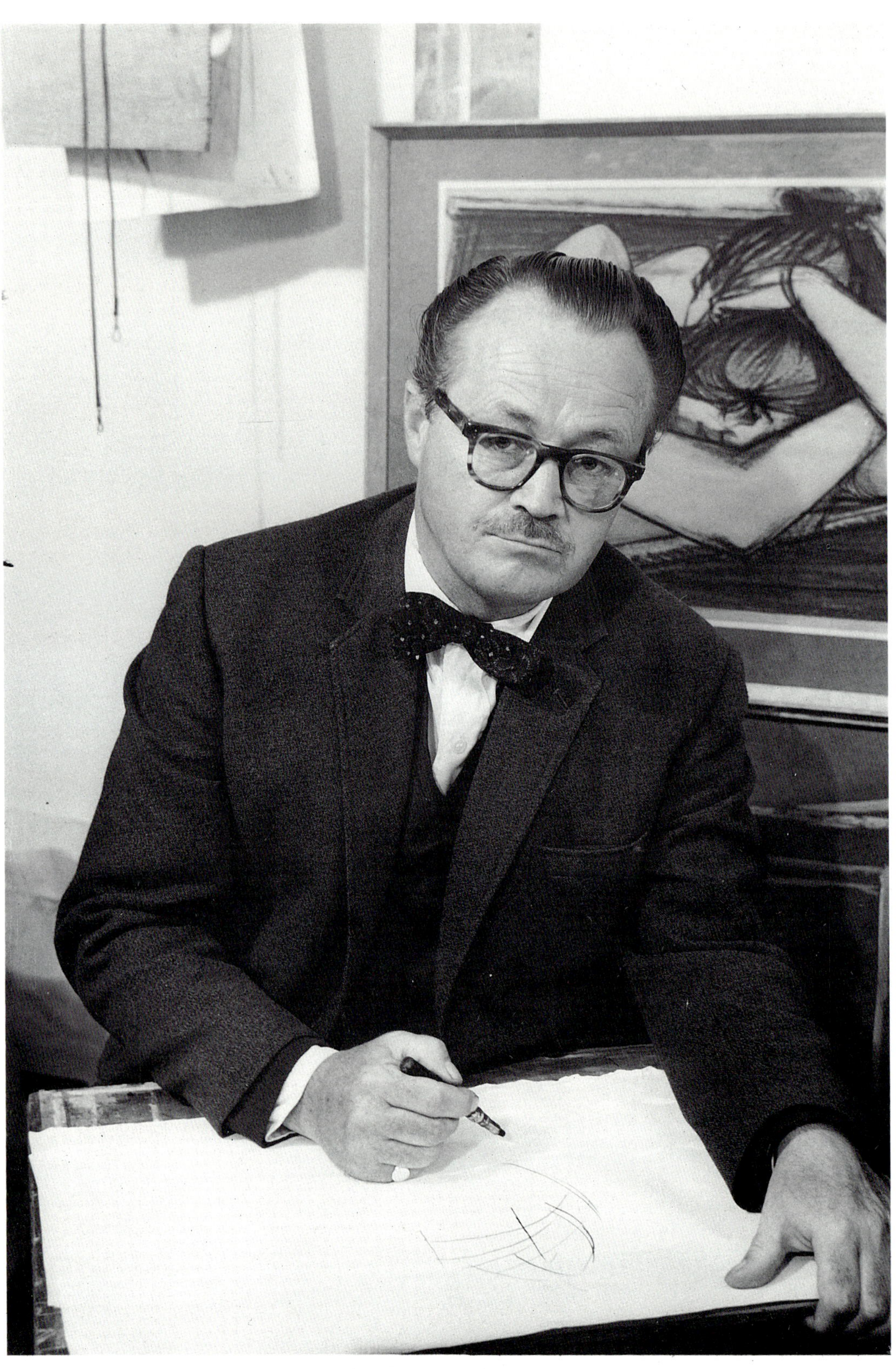

Press photograph from an early exhibition

Chronology

1919	30 May, Nigel Lambourne born in Croydon.
1919-c.24	Lives in Nottingham where his father, Herbert Lambourne, was then teaching at the University.
c.1924	Returns to Croydon, the family home.
1930-4	Attends Selhurst Grammar School.
1934-7	Studies at the Regent Street Polytechnic School of Art with Clifford Ellis and Stuart Tresilian, and at the Central School of Arts and Crafts with W. P. Robins in the evenings for etching.
1937-9	Studies at the Royal College of Art with Robert Austin – from whom he learned his metal engraving techniques – and Malcolm Osborne. There he meets Barbara Ward Standen as a fellow student.
1939-45	In France – which he knew from frequent childhood visits – at the outbreak of war. Enlists and serves in the British Army.
1942	4 September, marries Barbara Ward Standen, b.1919.
1945	20 February, Martyn, their only son, born.
1946-7	Completes degree course at the Royal College of Art. Awarded the Medal for Draughtsmanship and the Engraver and Lithographers Diploma. Teaches life classes at Isleworth Evening Institute whilst still at College. His earliest drawings and lithographs are of low life in the streets and cafés of Antwerp, small in scale, softly shaded, French in effect and with little evidence as yet of his resolute firmness of line. This came with a series of dance hall scenes of couples closely observed.
1947-	Work exhibited at the Colnaghi Gallery. Freelance practice includes press and editorial drawings for *Lilliput, The Leader,* and the J. Walter Thompson advertising agency, and children's book illustration for Elek, Dobson and Oxford University Press. At about this time he became a member of the Royal Society of Painter-Etchers and Engravers (A.R.E.) and also of the Senefelder Club.
1948	Work exhibited at the Leicester Galleries. Begins to teach illustration and engraving part-time at both the Regent Street Polytechnic and St Martin's Schools of Art.
1949	First one-man show of drawings, held at the Kensington Art Gallery. Illustrates Laurence Sterne: *A Sentimental Journey* [16 lithographs in 3 colours] for The Folio Society.
1950	Drawing expedition to Antwerp with the painter Clifford Hall. Exhibits with Edward Bawden and Lionel Bulmer at the Leicester Galleries, also included in 'Artists of Fame and Promise' at the same gallery. Prints in travelling exhibition shown at Chicago, New York and San Francisco.

1950-51 Joins a team including F. H. K. Henrion, Jock Kinnear and James Holland at the Central Office of Information, working on the Festival of Britain South Bank Exhibition. Lambourne's series of drawings of Victorian scientists was shown in the 'Dome of Discovery'. Murals at about this time for the buildings of the Central Office of Information and Design Research Unit. The large-scale dance hall couples are a major theme in his private work and the first bullfight drawings also date from these years.

1951-61 Teaches graphics and printmaking at Guildford College of Art, concurrently freelancing for the Ogilvie-Mather, Wasey, and Colman-Prentice-Varley advertising agencies. The major themes at the beginning of this period are still his monumental ladies paddling at the seaside and the vigorous pastel studies of bullfighters and fishermen: later came the first cycles of circus entertainers and strippers.

1951 Exhibits with Clifford Hall and John Buckland-Wright at the Colnaghi Gallery. Represented at the Leicester Galleries 'Artists of Fame and Promise' show.

1951-2 Holds one-man show at the Wilton Gallery.

1952-3 Prints in travelling exhibition/s to Chicago, New York and San Francisco.

1954 18 January-13 February, seven works in a show of contemporary English drawings at the Zwemmer Gallery. 6-27 May, two works included in the Leger Galleries exhibition entitled 'The New Realism in English Art': the other exhibitors being Andrews, Ardizzone, Ayrton, Freud, Gowing, Greaves, Hall, Herman, Hogarth, Lowry, Minton, Rogers, Smith, Spear and Spencer.
24 September-14 October, one-man show 'Typical Examples of Recent Work' at the Zwemmer Gallery. Illustrates Daniel Defoe: *Moll Flanders* [19 line drawings] for The Folio Society. Death of John Buckland-Wright.

1954-7 Works purchased for the following public collections: the Museum of Modern Art, New York; the National Galleries of Australia, New Zealand and Canada; the Arts Council and the Contemporary Art Society.

1956 8-29 February, 'Bullfight and Other Drawings' – one-man show at the Zwemmer Gallery, from which 30 subjects were later shown at the Chapel Bar Gallery in Nottingham because of his local connection: Nottingham Castle Museum purchased three fine drawings.

1957 26 November-4 January 1958, well represented in the Zwemmer Gallery 'New Editions: Colour Prints' exhibition.

1958 Represented in Zwemmer Gallery's collective exhibition.

1959 5-27 February, one-man show of drawings at the Zwemmer Gallery. Illustrates Guy de Maupassant: *Short Stories* [14 drawings] for The Folio Society.

1959/60 Exhibits with Albert Garrett and Clifford Hall at the Wilton Gallery. Dominant themes from now on include acrobats and strippers – Marseille a favourite location – unconventionally observed torsos and geriatric studies, and a smaller group of rock surface landscapes made in quarries or along the Gower coast.

1961 Nigel Lambourne: *Drawing People in Action*, ed. Mervyn Levy (London: Studio Books/New York: Watson-Guptill). Illustrates Liam O'Flaherty: *The Informer* [8 lithographs] for The Folio Society.

1962 Appointed as a part-time lecturer in illustration in the Faculty of Graphic Design at Leicester Polytechnic (until 1972).

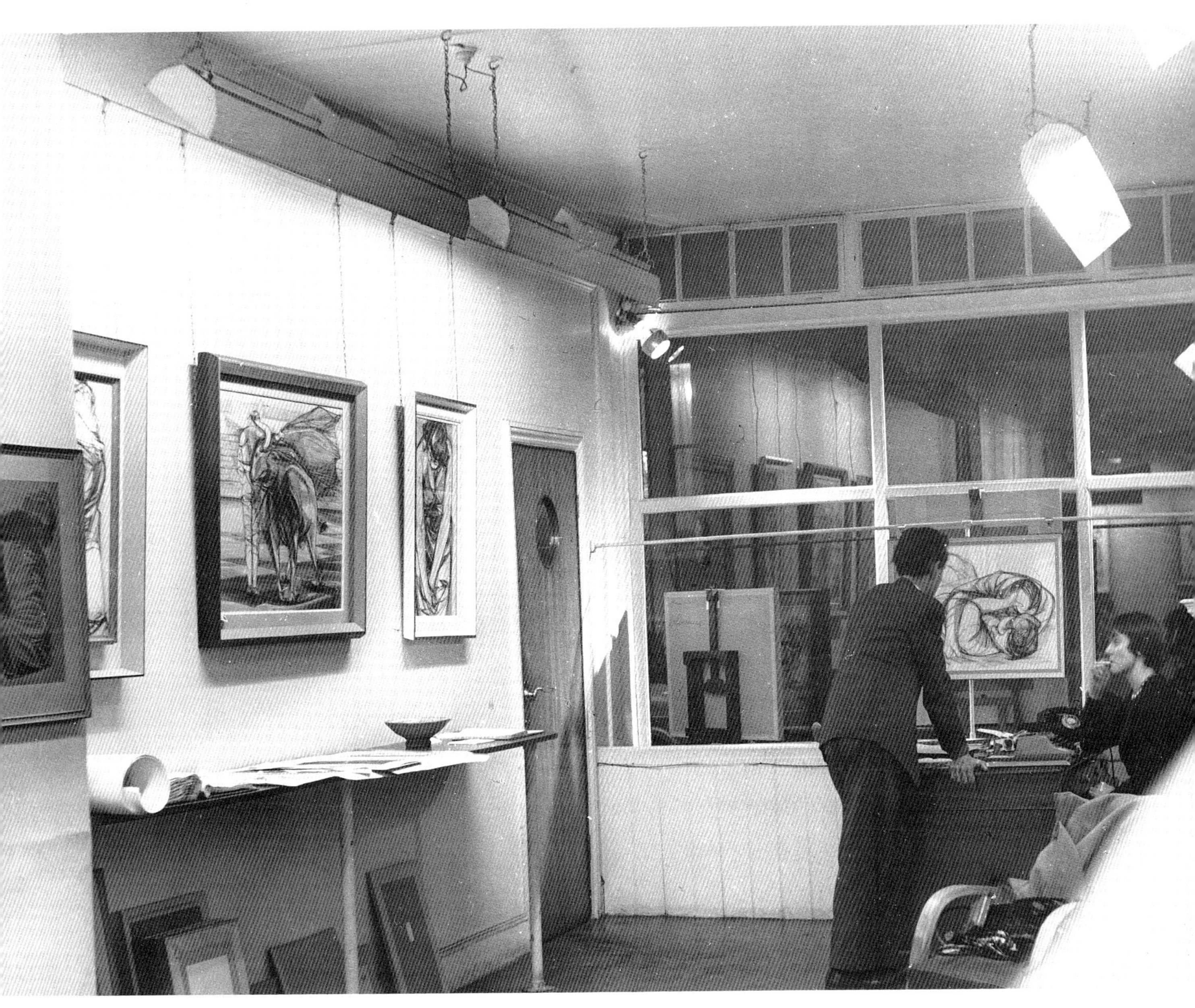

Nigel Lambourne exhibition, Zwemmer Gallery, 1954 [Zwemmer archive]

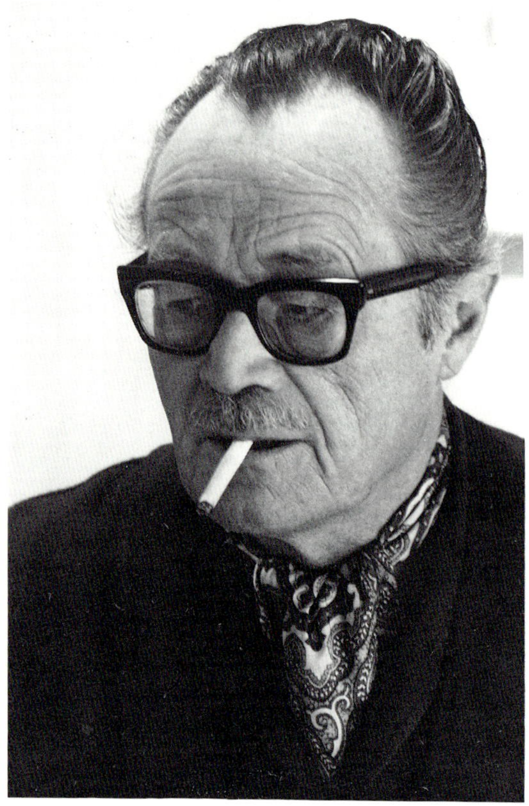

Portrait, October 1981 [photo: Ian Wood]

1963	*Rembrandt van Rijn: paintings, drawings and etchings,* selected and introduced by Nigel Lambourne (The Folio Society).
1963-4	Book illustrations commissioned by the Department of Education & Science, Wellington, New Zealand.
1964	Illustrates Feodor Dostoyevsky: *The Brothers Karamazov* [24 drawings] for The Folio Society. Vacation spent in Turkey.
1965	*Dog Years,* Ralph Manheim's translation of Günter Grass: *Hundejahre,* published. This inspired a vast cycle of drawings on the scarecrow theme. *Renoir: paintings, drawings, lithographs and etchings,* selected and introduced by Nigel Lambourne (The Folio Society). Further vacation in Turkey.
1966	Barbara Lambourne is appointed a full-time lecturer in the Faculty of Fashion & Textiles at Leicester (until 1984).
1967	Illustrates Franz Kafka: *The Trial* [41 photogrammes] for The Folio Society. The Lambournes buy and move into a Georgian house at 3 The Cross, Enderby, Leicestershire.
1968	Commissioned to prepare drawings for James Joyce's *Ulysses;* one of several projects which remained unpublished, including Marlowe's *Dr Faustus* (Leipziger Presse, 1971) and Ovid's *Amores* (The Folio Society, c.1977).
1969	*Albrecht Dürer: paintings, drawings and prints,* selected and introduced by Nigel Lambourne (The Folio Society). Illustrates Publius Vergilius Maro: *The Georgics* [5 soft-ground etchings by direct-plate process] for The Folio Society.

c.1970 Discovered Kleist's *Über das Marionettentheater*, which yielded imagery which occupied him on and off for the next fifteen years.

1971 One-man show at Editions Graphiques Gallery. Represented by three drawings for the ancient Japanese folk tale *The Spirit of Sakura* at 'Figura 1', Internationale Buchkunst-Ausstellung, Leipzig.

1972 Resigned from Leicester Polytechnic, and undertook no further teaching although he was retained as an external examinations assessor by other colleges. Wilfred Owen: *Ten War Poems*, illustrated by Nigel Lambourne and Paul Peter Piech (Willow Dene: Taurus Press).

1973 Death of Clifford Hall.

1974 Illustrates Anton Chekhov: *Short Stories* [8 aquatints reproduced by collotype] for The Folio Society.

1976 Exhibits his retrospective work 1969-76, with Ann Hewson (widow of Clifford Hall) at the Belgrave Gallery.

1976-7 Drawings for posters and leaflets for the Haymarket Theatre, Leicester, where a small exhibition of Lambourne's work was also held.

1977 Illustrates James Tucker: *Ralph Rashleigh* [16 line drawings] for The Folio Society.

1983 Illustrates Benjamin Disraeli: *Sybil* [17 line drawings] for The Folio Society.

1984 Moves to Dean Cottage, Oakhill, near Bath.

1988 Travel to Turkey and Provence. 12 December, died at Oakhill.

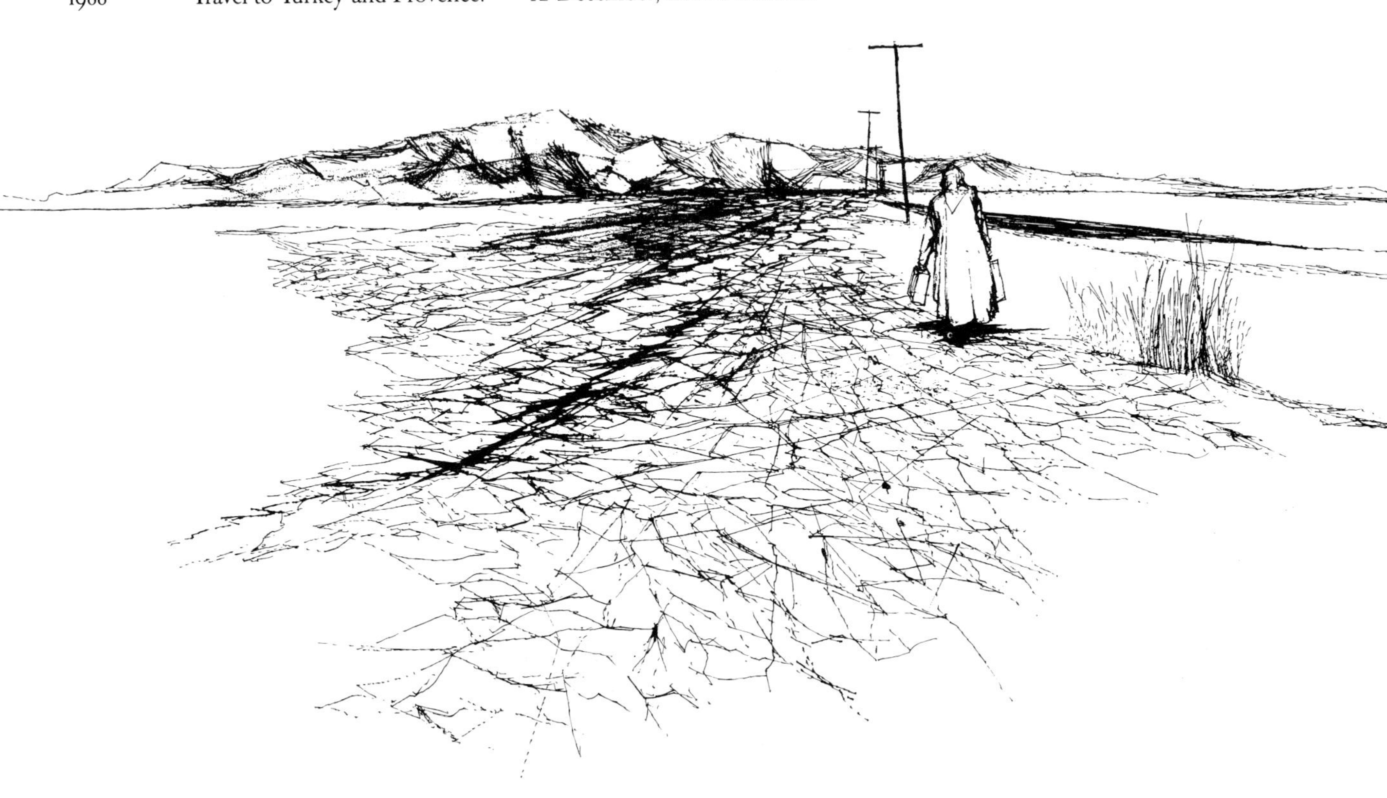

Anatolia, 1965/77 [whereabouts unknown]

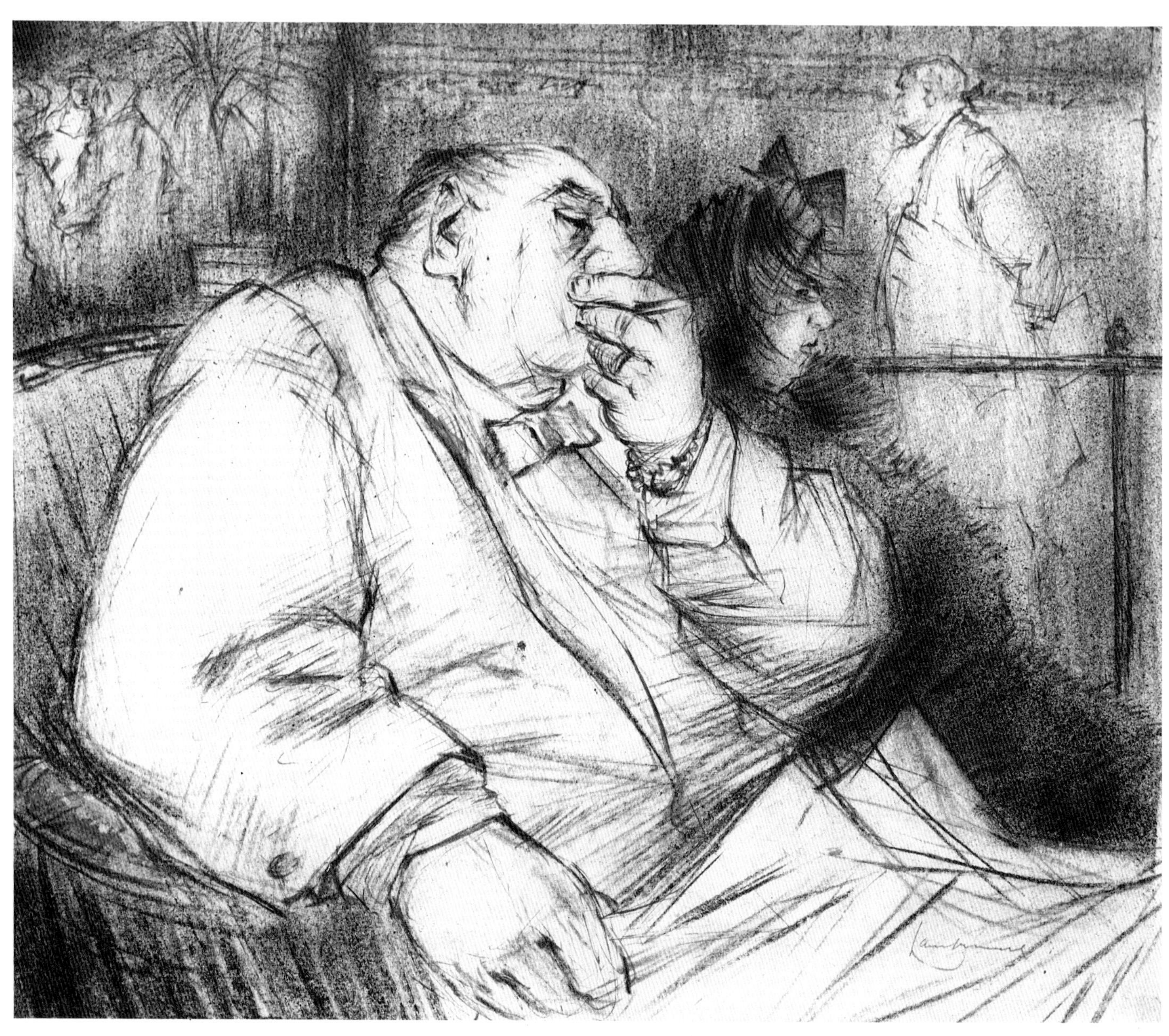

[No. 3] *At the Theatre*

Catalogue

1 **Portrait of 'Rusty' M.** 1947

Lithograph
230 x 205 mm
Signed: Lambourne
Inscribed on stone: NL, 1947 'Rusty' M., Panton Street W1
Ann Hall collection

2 **In a Café** c.1947/8

Mixed media
265 x 365 mm
No signature or date
Nigel Lambourne Estate

3 **At the Theatre** c.1947/8

Mixed media
255 x 310 mm
Signed lower r: Lambourne, undated
Nigel Lambourne Estate

4 **Streetwalker, Antwerp** c.1949

Black chalks and greyish splatter
520 x 385 mm
Signed top 1: Lambourne, undated
[A later version exists as a drawing dated 1972/74]
Nigel Lambourne Estate

5 **The Financial Body** 1950 or earlier

Pastel
300 x 245 mm
Signed top 1: Lambourne
[Shown at the Leicester Galleries 'Artists of Fame and Promise' exhibition in 1950]
Lowell Libson collection

6 **Lovers** 1950

Conté, pastel
465 x 755 mm
Signed lower r: Lambourne
Nottingham City Museums; Castle Museum and Art Gallery
Acc. no: 1956 94

7 **Bullfight VI** c.1950

Conté, charcoal and pastel
970 x 745 mm
Signed top r: Lambourne
Nottingham City Museums; Castle Museum and Art Gallery
Acc. no: 1956 95

8 **Horse and Bull** c.1950

Conté, charcoal, pastel and watercolour
950 x 750 mm
Signed lower l: Lambourne
Nottingham City Museums; Castle Museum and Art Gallery
Acc. no: 1956 96

9 **Bullfighter** c.1950

Pastel
675 x 495 mm
Signed centre l: Lambourne
[One of ten pictures entitled 'Bullfight' exhibited in 1956]
Private collection, Bristol

10 **Matador** early 1950s

Pastel
410 x 635 mm
Signed lower r: Nigel Lambourne, undated
Nigel Lambourne Estate

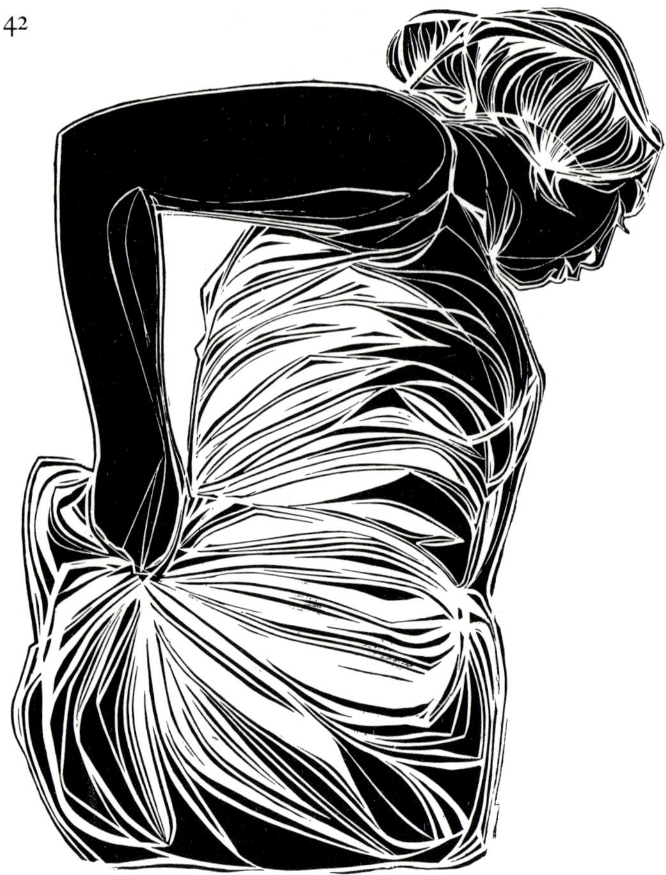

[No. 15] *Paddling*

11 **The Paddlers** early 1950s

Pen and wash
760 x 550 mm
Signed lower r: Nigel Lambourne, not dated
Nigel Lambourne Estate

12 **A Paddler** early 1950s

Chalk, pastel and watercolour
870 x 600 mm
Signed lower l: Nigel Lambourne, not dated
Nigel Lambourne Estate

13 **Drawing from Seated Model** early 1950s

Charcoal, chalk and pencil
460 x 340 mm
No signature or date
Nigel Lambourne Estate

14 **Paddler** 1951

Aquatint
315 x 230 mm
Signed at foot: Nigel Lambourne 1951
Inscribed: 4/9, iv st.
Nigel Lambourne Estate

15 **Paddling** not later than 1954

Linocut
385 x 280 mm
Signed: Nigel Lambourne, undated
Inscribed: 'Paddling', 9/xii
Nigel Lambourne Estate

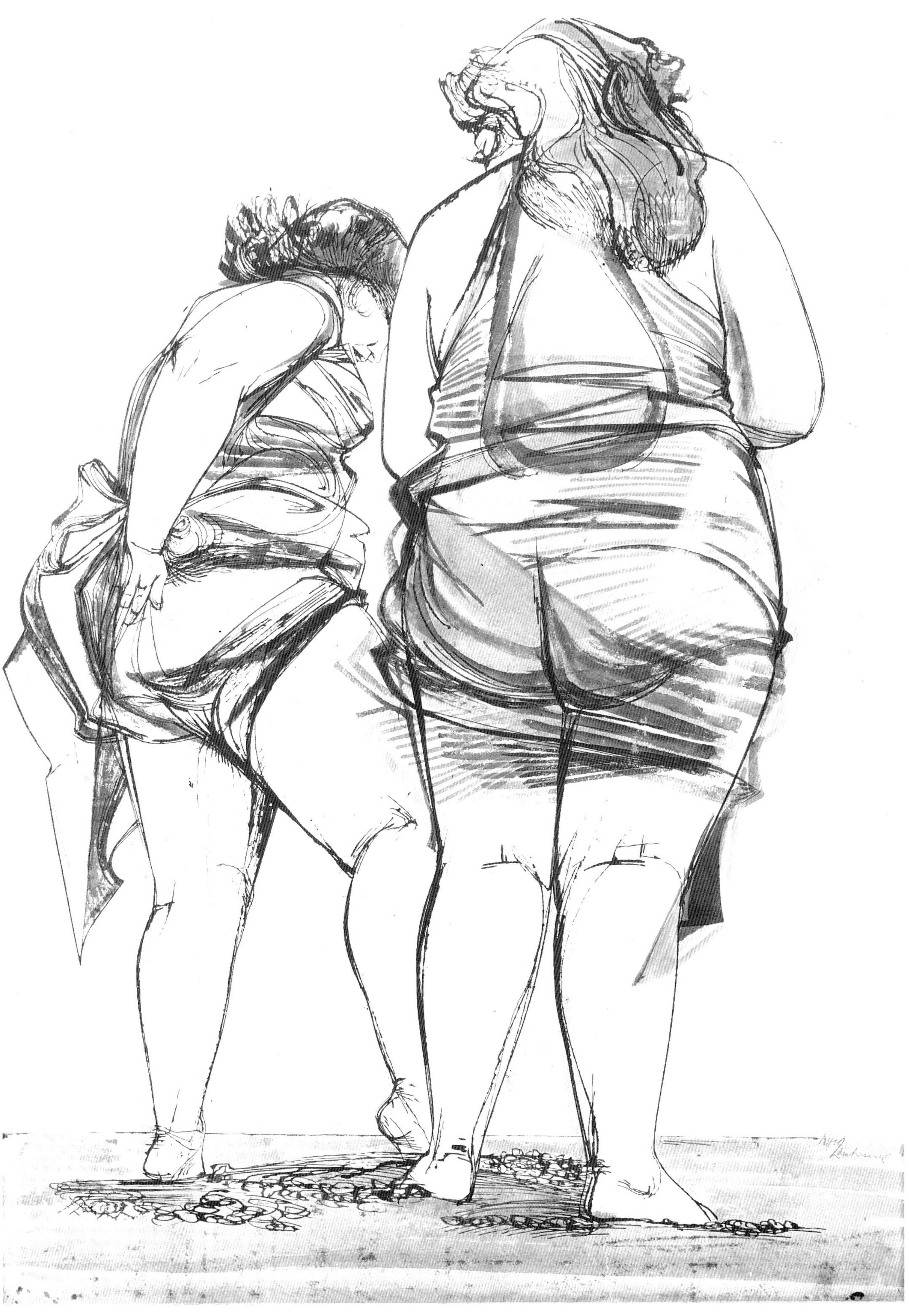

[No. 11] *The Paddlers*

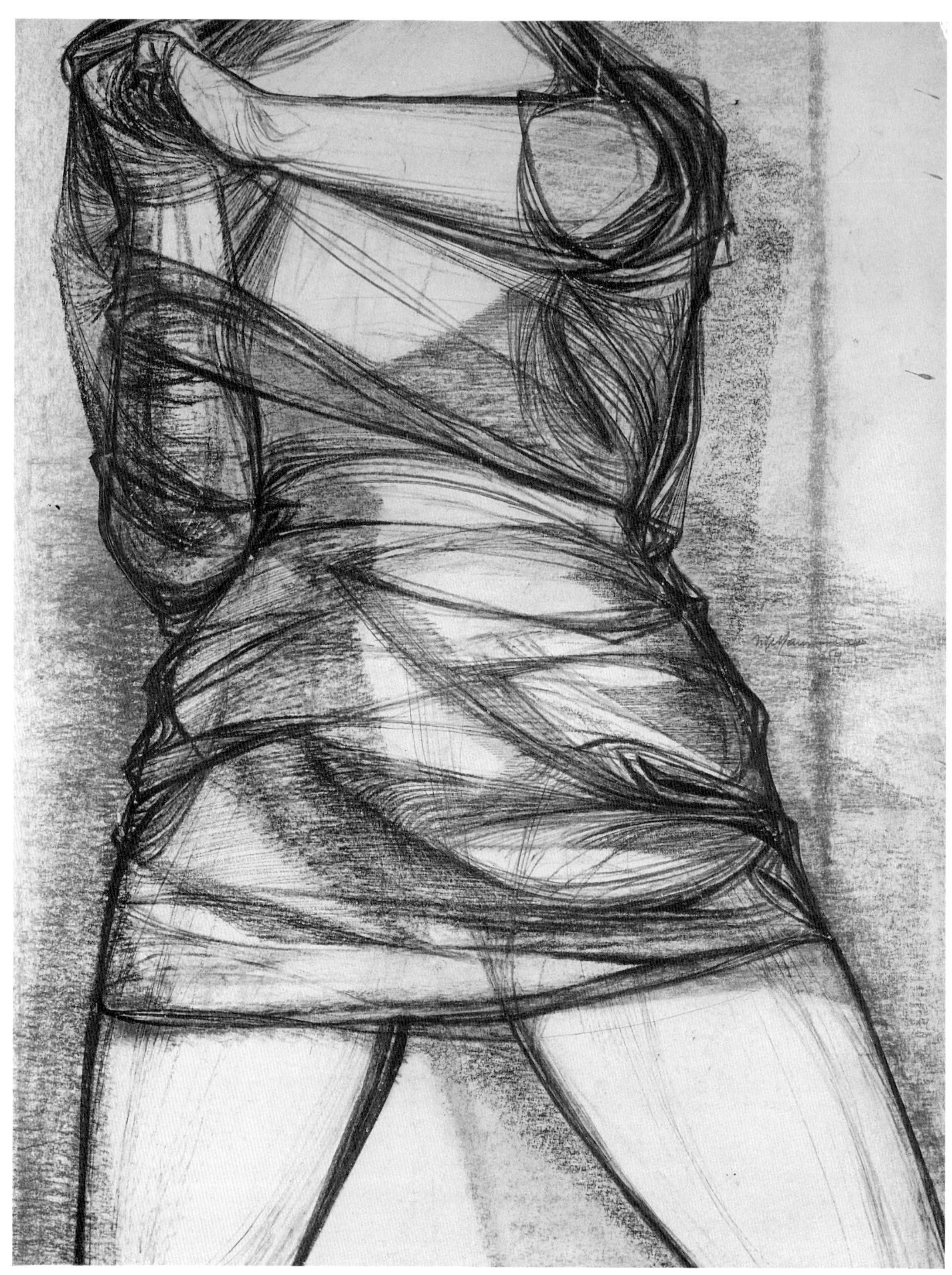

[No. 19] *Torso with Clasped Hands*

16 **Seated Figures** not later than 1954

Chalk, pastel and watercolour
530 x 740 mm
Signature and date erased top r, and re-signed: Nigel Lambourne
Nigel Lambourne Estate

17 **The Nightdress** not later than 1954

Mixed media
785 x 560 mm
Signed top r: Lambourne, undated
Ann Hall collection

18 **The Bullfight** c.1953

Crayon and wash
920 x 710 mm
Signed in pencil lower l: Lambourne, not dated
[Not shown in exhibition but reproduced in catalogue]
National Art Gallery, New Zealand
Accession no: 1957/15/3

19 **Torso with Clasped Hands** 1954

Chalk, pastel and crayon, with pencil tracing-down marks
680 x 530 mm
Signed centre r: Nigel Lambourne 1954
Nigel Lambourne Estate

20 **Frontal Torso: Raised Arms pulling Garment over Head** 1954

Aquatint
455 x 305 mm
Signed: Nigel Lambourne
Inscribed: 5/7 for Clifford, Dec. '54
Ann Hall collection

21 **Sailors** 1950s

Charcoal, pastel, chalk and wash
535 x 725 mm
Signed lower l: Nigel Lambourne, not dated
Private collection

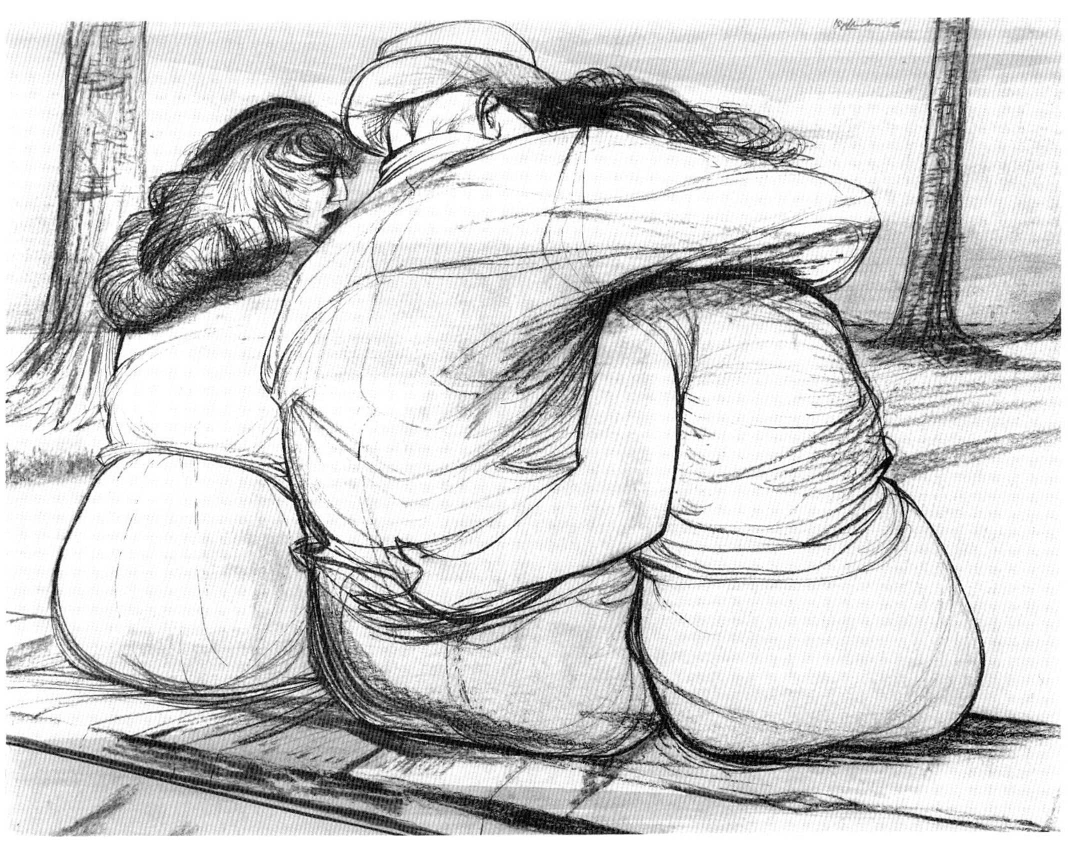

[No. 16] *Seated Figures*

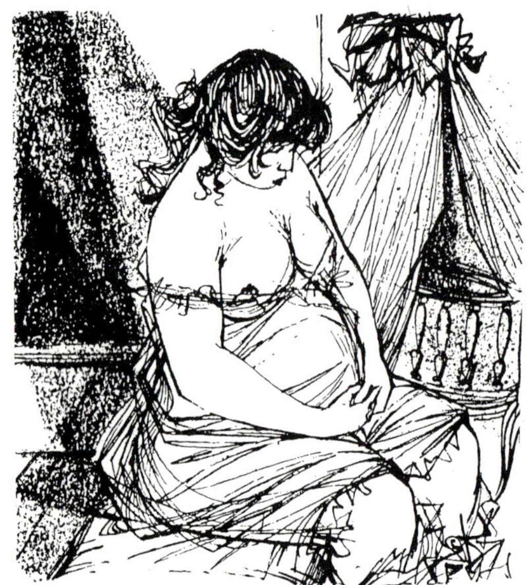

Line illustrations for Moll Flanders, 1954

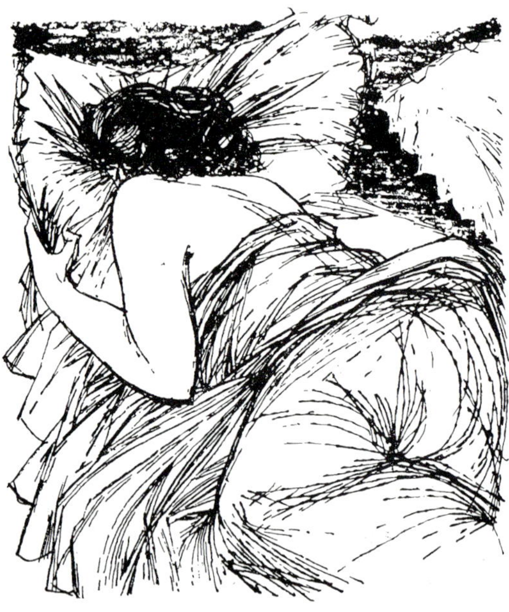

22 **Mother and Child** 1950s

Chalk, pastel and watercolour
735 x 520 mm
Signed lower l: Nigel Lambourne, not dated
Nigel Lambourne Estate

23 **Undressing** 1950s

Chalk and pastel
680 x 455 mm
Signed lower r: Lambourne, not dated
Nigel Lambourne Estate

24 **Paddler with Folded Arms** 1950s

Linocut
625 x 315 mm
No signature or date
Nigel Lambourne Estate

25 **Marathon Dancers/Fantasy** [iii] 1950s

Chalk, pastel and watercolour
760 x 505 mm
Original signature visible lower l: Nigel Lambourne
Signed again lower r: Nigel Lambourne 1973 [a later reworking?]
Inscribed on back: Marathon Dancers/Fantasy [iii]
Nigel Lambourne Estate

26 **Bullfighter** probably 1950s, although no first edition print has been traced

Linocut
530 x 375 mm
Signed lower r: Nigel Lambourne '74, trial ii/9
Nigel Lambourne Estate

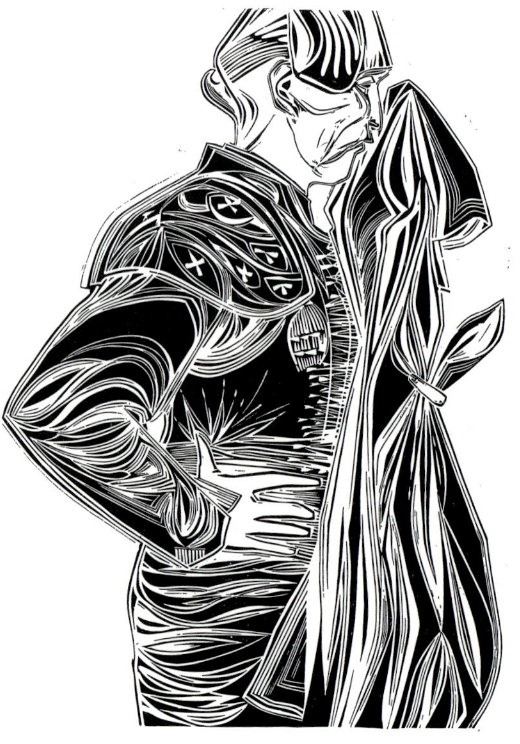

[No. 26] *Bullfighter*

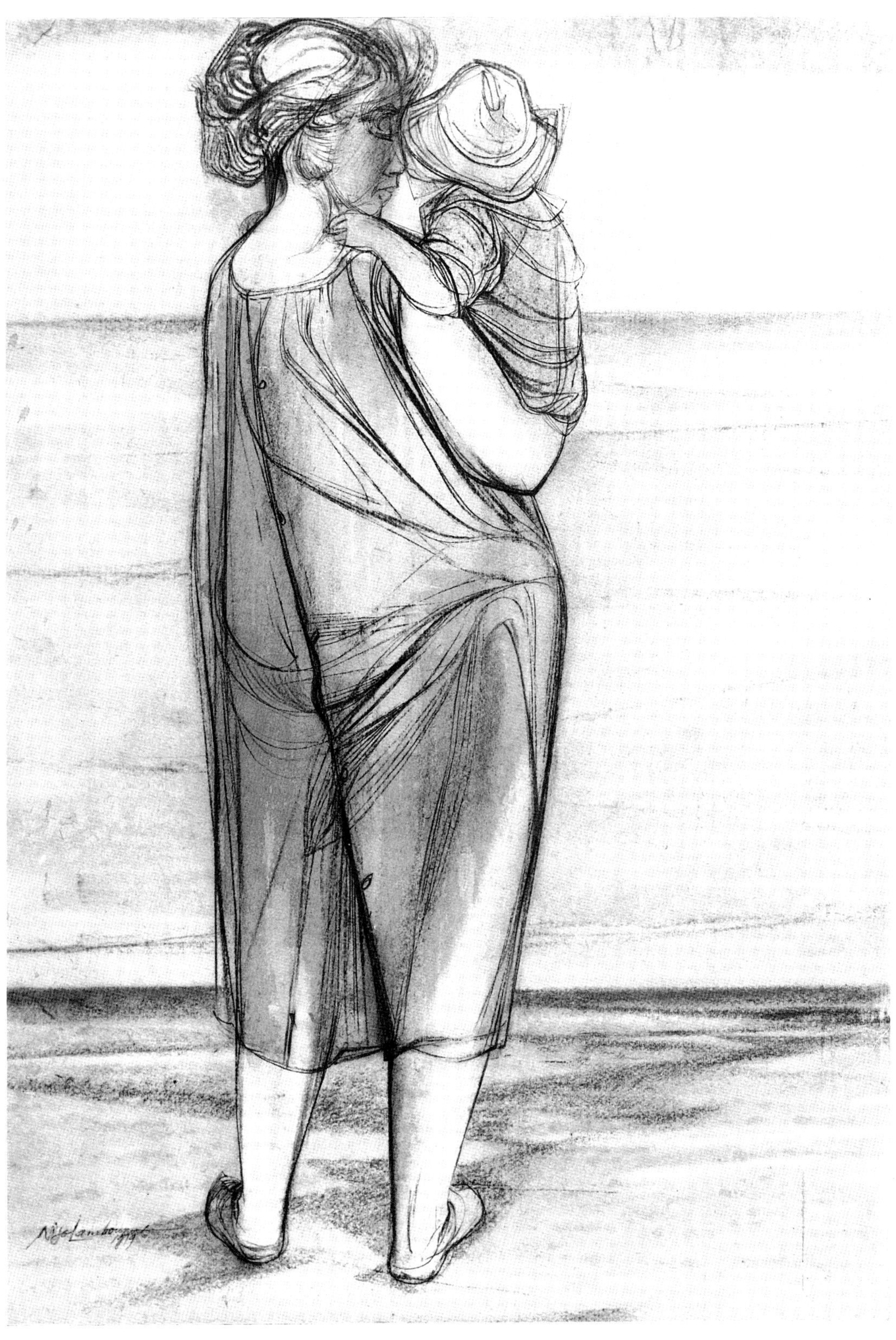

[No. 22] *Mother and Child*

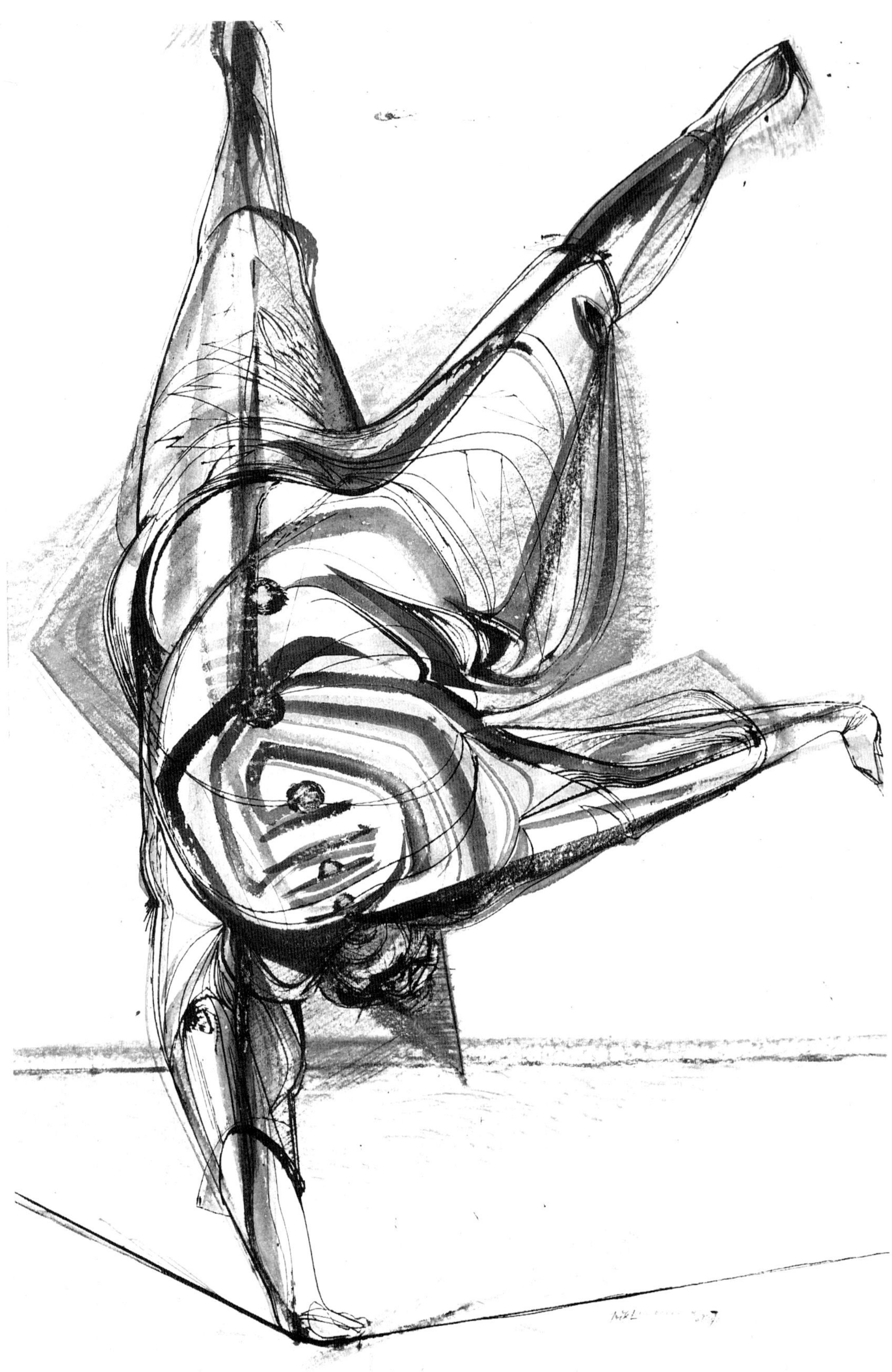

[No. 27] *Acrobat*

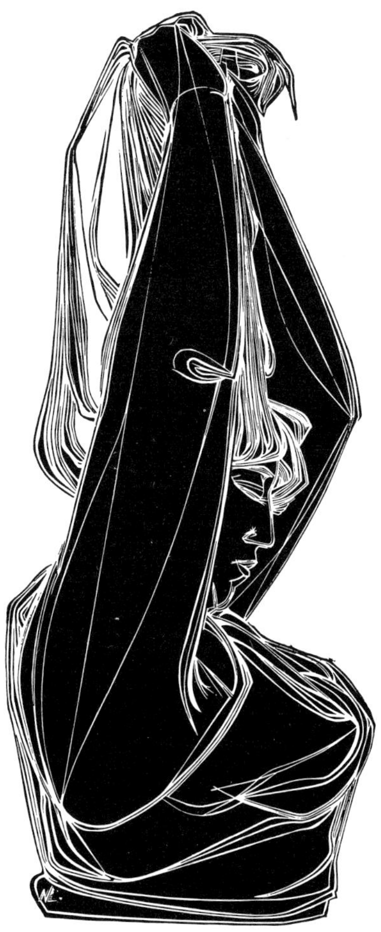

[No. 30] *Raised Arms*, linocut

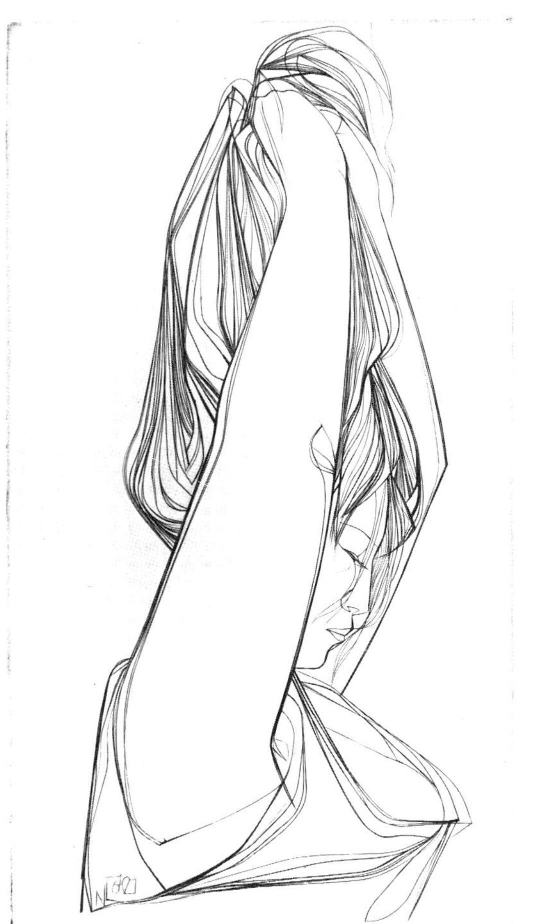

[No. 31] *Raised Arms*, copper engraving

27 **Acrobat** probably 1950s

Ink, pastel and watercolour
725 x 480 mm
Signed lower r: Nigel Lambourne, 1970
[previous date obliterated]
Inscribed on back: Acrobat Sept 1971
Nigel Lambourne Estate

28 **Couple** late 1950s or early 1960s

Chalk and watercolour
700 x 495 mm
Not signed or dated
Nigel Lambourne Estate

29 **Girl with Guitar** early 1960s

Pen and ink on grey paper
460 x 380 mm
Unsigned and undated sketch
Nigel Lambourne Estate

30 **Raised Arms (Hairdressing)** early 1960s

Linocut
530 x 220 mm
Signed in block: NL
Signed beneath: Nigel Lambourne, not dated
Private collection

31 **Raised Arms (Hairdressing)** 1962

Copper engraving
303 x 170 mm
Signed: Nigel Lambourne 1962
Inscribed: 3/2 (ii), for Clifford & Ann, May 1962
Ann Hall collection

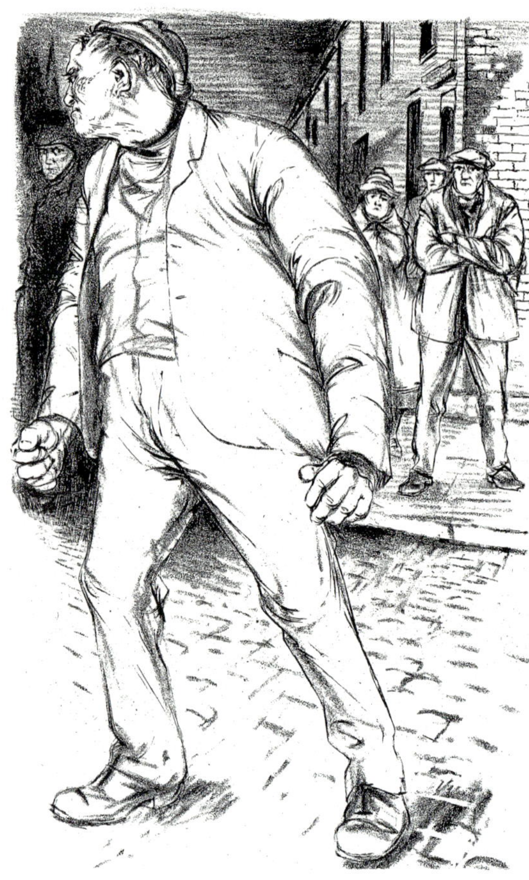

Illustration for The Informer, 1961

32 **Nude with Raised Arm** 1965 or earlier

Pen and ink and watercolour
510 x 355 mm
Signed lower r: Nigel Lambourne
Inscribed in pencil lower r: for Clifford, for Ann, Dec 1965
Ann Hall collection

33 **Curled-up Figure** 1965

Black and white chalks and pastel on mid green paper
510 x 700 mm
Signed: Nigel Lambourne and dated 1965 [or possibly 1966]
Inscribed: for Clifford and Ann, December 1966
Ann Hall collection

34 **Gower Coast [i]** mid 1960s

Pastel, ink and watercolour
420 x 650 mm
No signature or date
Nigel Lambourne Estate

35 **Gower Coast [ii]** mid 1960s

Mixed media
490 x 1005 mm
No signature or date
Nigel Lambourne Estate

36 **Dog Years [i]** 1965 or later

Line with wash
750 x 520 mm
Signed lower l: Nigel Lambourne, not dated
Inscribed on back: 'Dog Years' [i]
Nigel Lambourne Estate

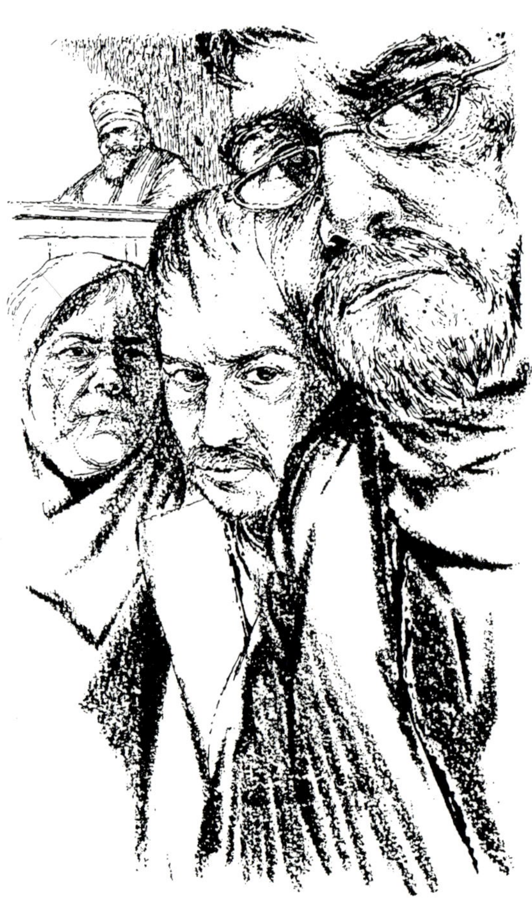

Illustration for The Brothers Karamazov, 1964

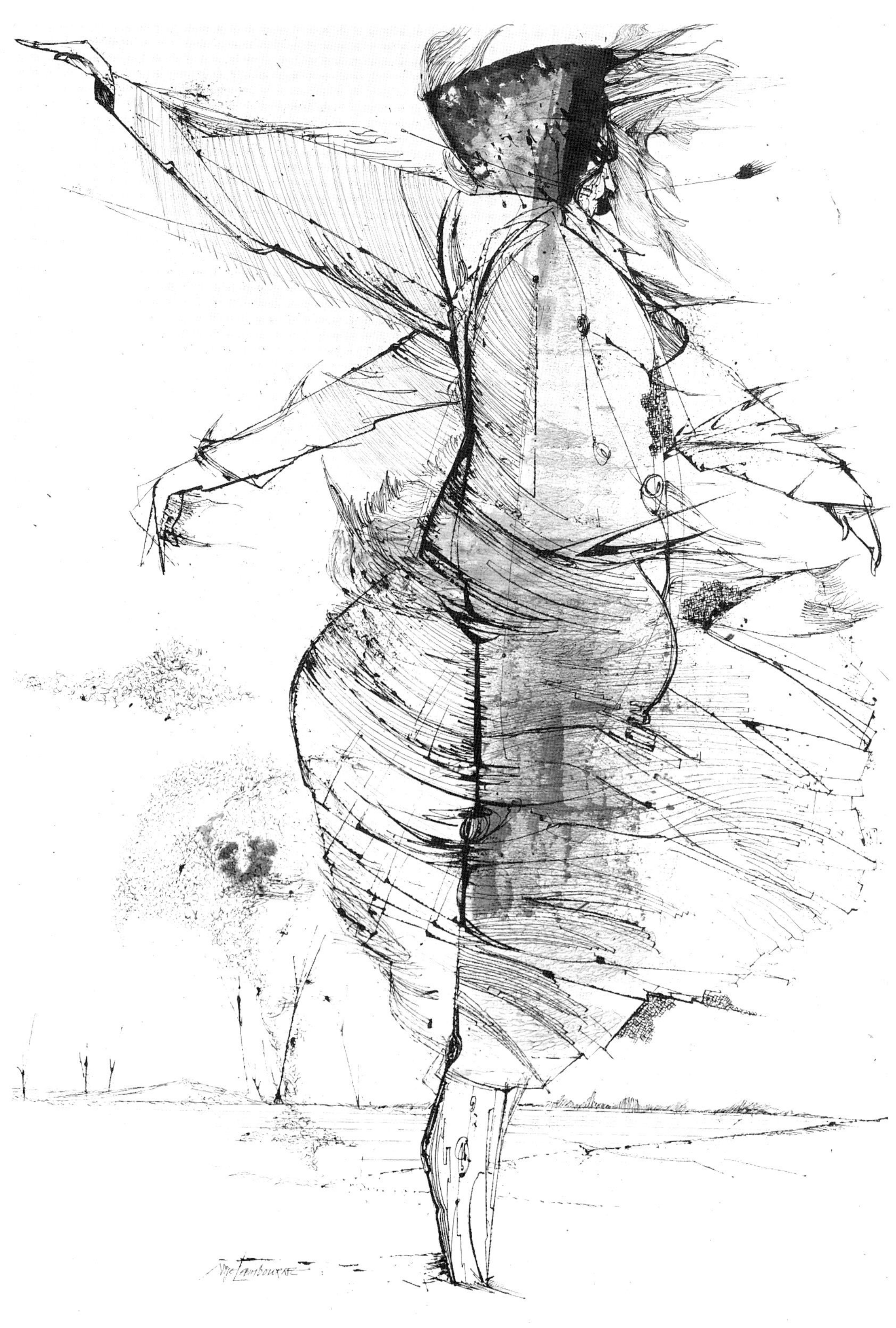

[No. 36] *Dog Years* [*i*]

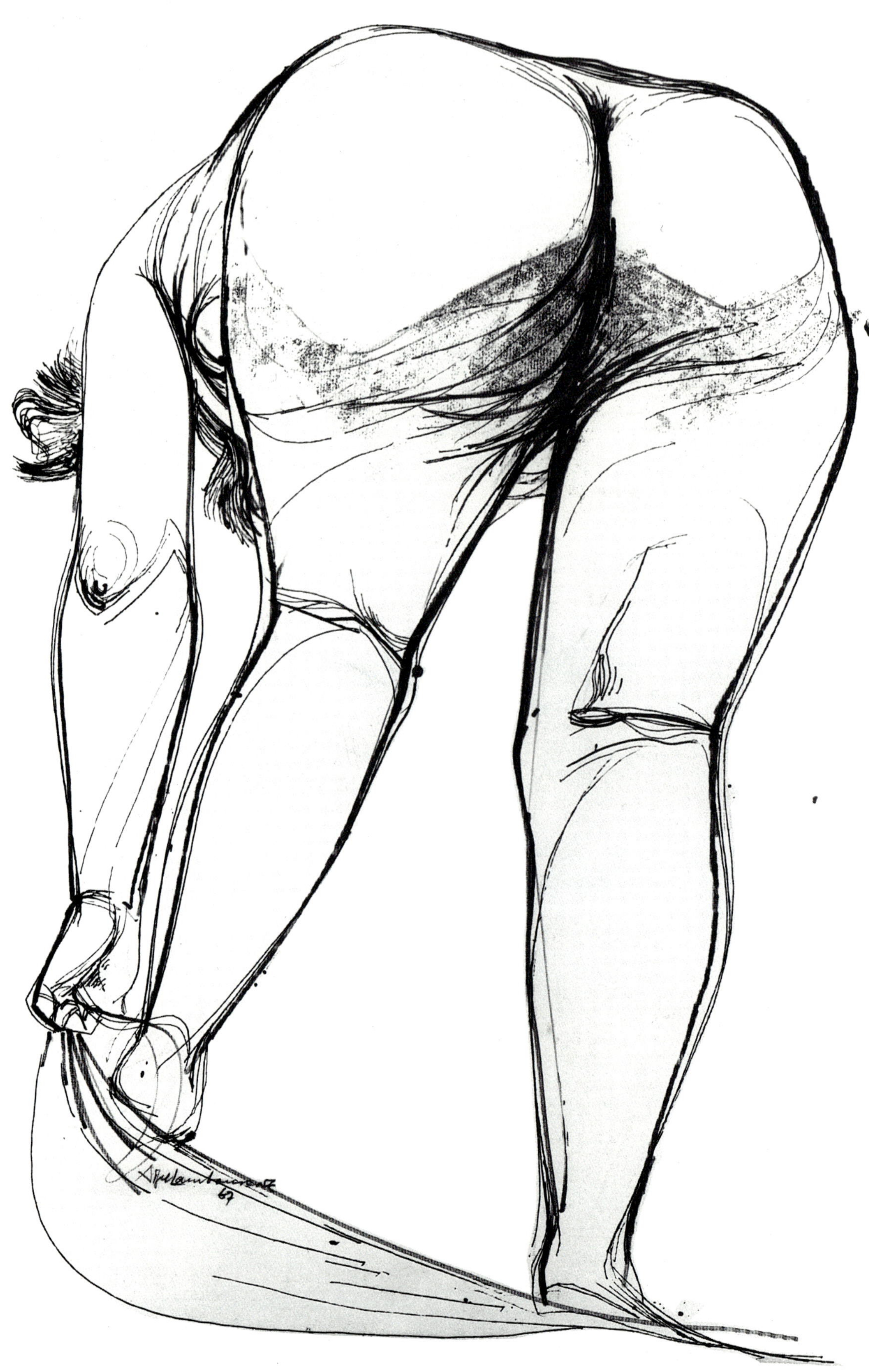

[No. 39] *Figure with Towel*

37 **Rock Stratification, Gower** 1966

Black pen and brush, over resist ground
760 x 485 mm
Signed at edge l: Nigel Lambourne
Dated at foot: Sept/Dec '66
Ann Hall collection

38 **Life Study** 1967

Black chalk on pink paper
665 x 465 mm
Signed lower edge r: Nigel Lambourne 1967
Private collection

39 **Figure with Towel** 1967

Ink, spirit marker and dry-transfer texture
600 x 425 mm
Signed lower l: Nigel Lambourne '67
Nigel Lambourne Estate

40 **Scarecrow Image from the Text of 'Dog Years' by Günter Grass** 1968

Pen and indian ink
645 x 540 mm
Signed lower r edge: Nigel Lambourne '68
Private collection

Linocut for a bookplate, undated [whereabouts unknown]

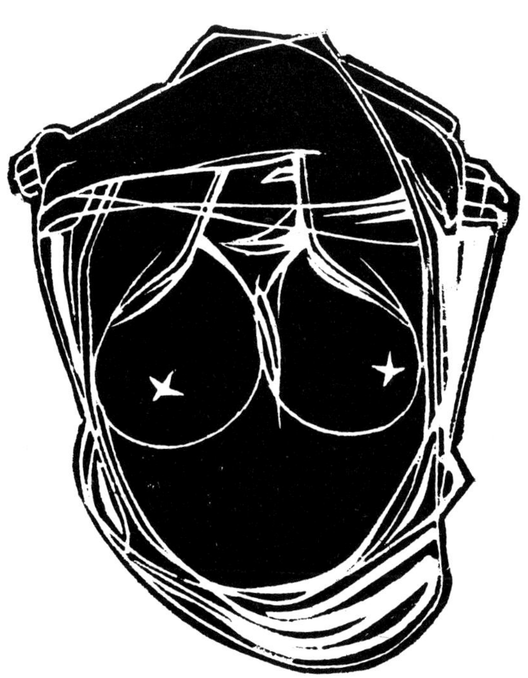

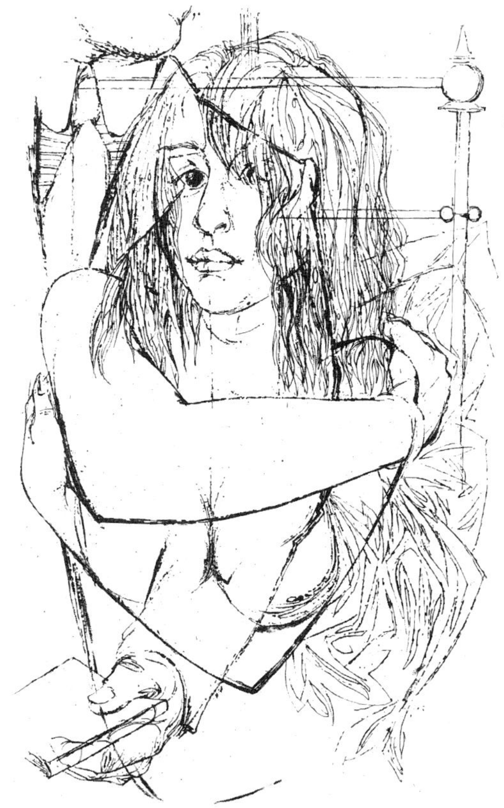

[No. 41] *Bloom bringing Molly Letter & Breakfast*

41 **Bloom bringing Molly Letter & Breakfast,** mounted together with an annotated preliminary study for the same subject c.1968
Unpublished book illustration to James Joyce: *Ulysses*
Pen and indian ink
335 x 210 mm
Unsigned, not dated
Private collection

42 **Bloom, Sea-shore & Gertie** c.1968

Unpublished book illustration to James Joyce: *Ulysses*
Two preliminary sketches and a nearly complete illustration; respectively in pencil, Conté crayon, and pen
315 x 210 mm [pencil], 335 x 215 mm [Conté], 305 x 200 mm [pen]
All unsigned, not dated
Pencil drawing is annotated: Bloom, sea-shore & Gertie; ± 5 Drgs lost after Brian Rawson's death
[This project had been initiated by the Folio Society, where Brian Rawson had been editor: NL understood that it had foundered on copyright considerations]
Private collection

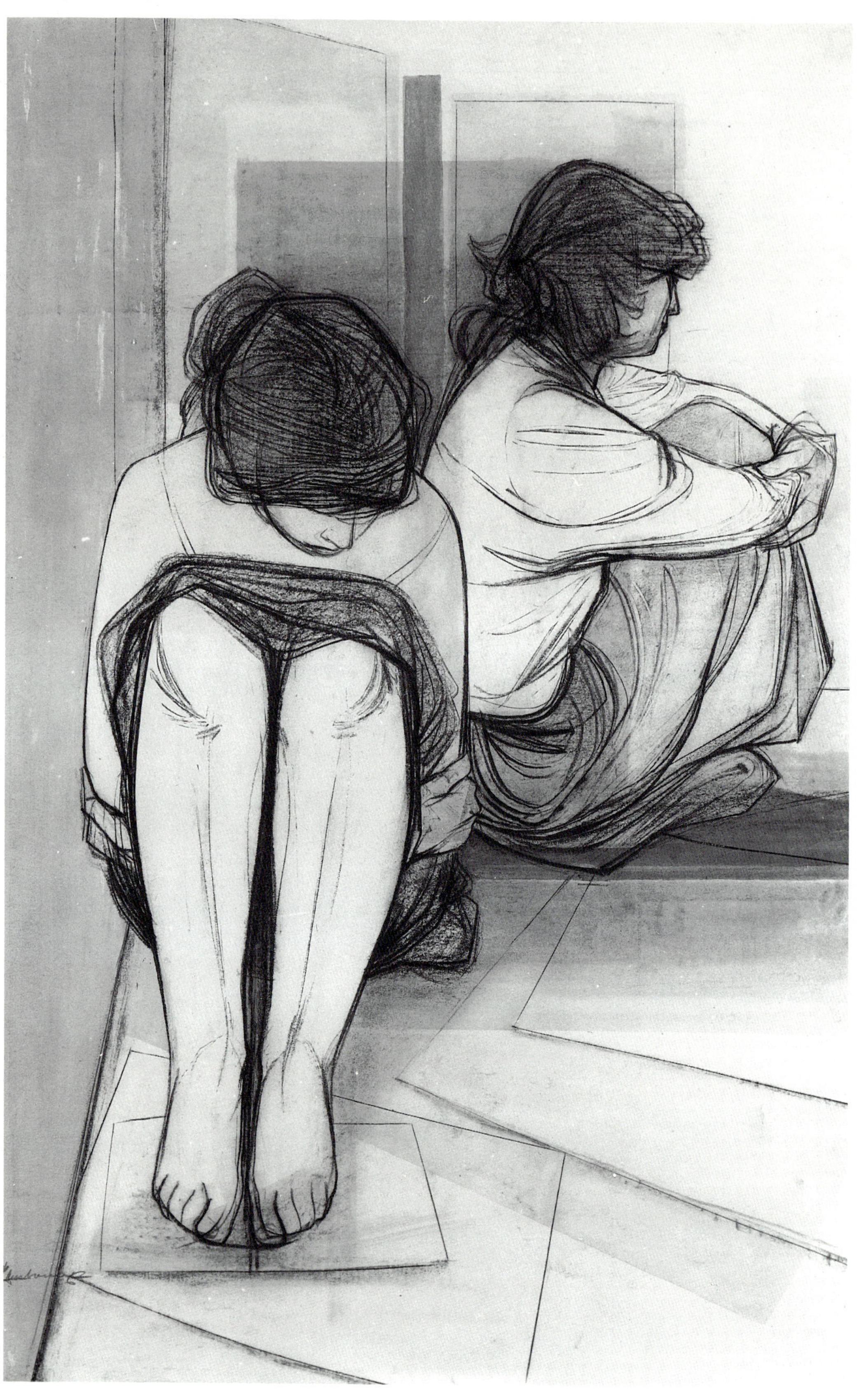

[No. 55] *Student's Concert*, 1972/4

43 **Moll Flanders** 1968-70

Brown-grey chalk with spirit markers in fawn, brown and greys, and pen and indian ink
535 x 255 mm
Signed top r: Nigel Lambourne '68-, [amended] '69-70, [amended in pencil] '76 last
Inscribed top r: 'Moll' 4, frontis x 2 and in pencil lower r: frontis Moll Flanders for CE?
[The Folio Society *Moll Flanders,* first published 1954, had been entirely reset in 1965 retaining NL's original drawings. The frontispiece is not one of his best drawings, and this may have been a proposal for substitution in the 4th impression, addressed to Charles Ede, the society's founder-director.]
Private collection

44 **Dancer, Istanbul** 1969

Pen and ink, and resist
750 x 460 mm
Signed lower centre: Nigel Lambourne
Inscribed on back: Dancer: Istanbul Aug '69
[following the visits of 1964 and 1965]
Nigel Lambourne Estate

45 **Quarry, Bethesda** 1960s

Ink and watercolour
760 x 495 mm
Signed: Nigel Lambourne
Ann Hall collection

46 **Bird Image** late 1960s

Pen and ink
635 x 460 mm
Signed lower l: Nigel Lambourne, undated
[This drawing is dated in relation to Lambourne's interest in Leonard Baskin's concurrent work with Ted Hughes]
Nigel Lambourne Estate

47 **Students' Concert** 1970s or earlier

Linocut
645 x 480 mm
No signature or date
[See also 55]
Nigel Lambourne Estate

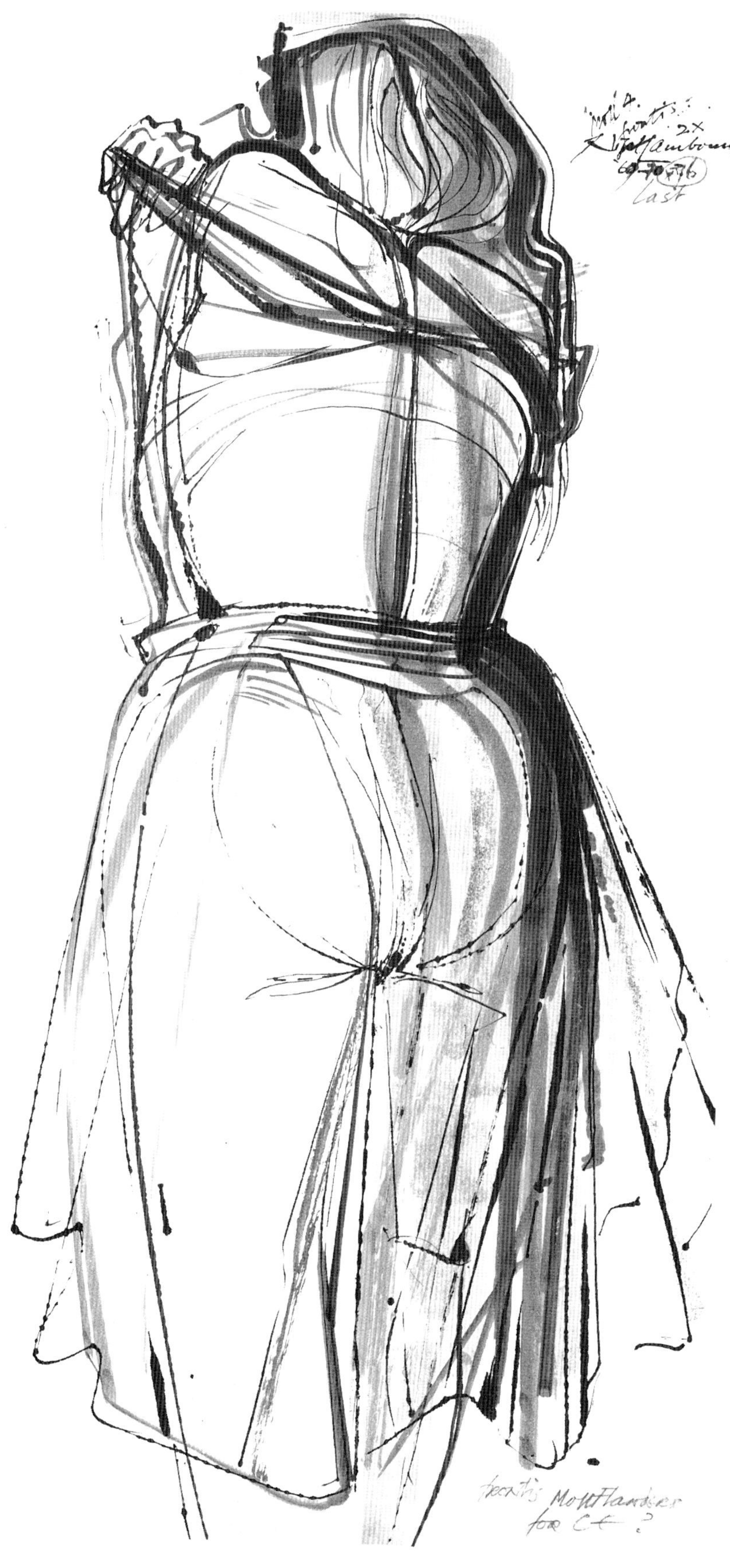

[No. 43] *Moll Flanders*

48 Dancer or Gymnast Holding Sphere early 1970s

Chalk and dry brushwork
675 x 435 mm
Signed at edge 1: Nigel Lambourne, undated
Nigel Lambourne Estate

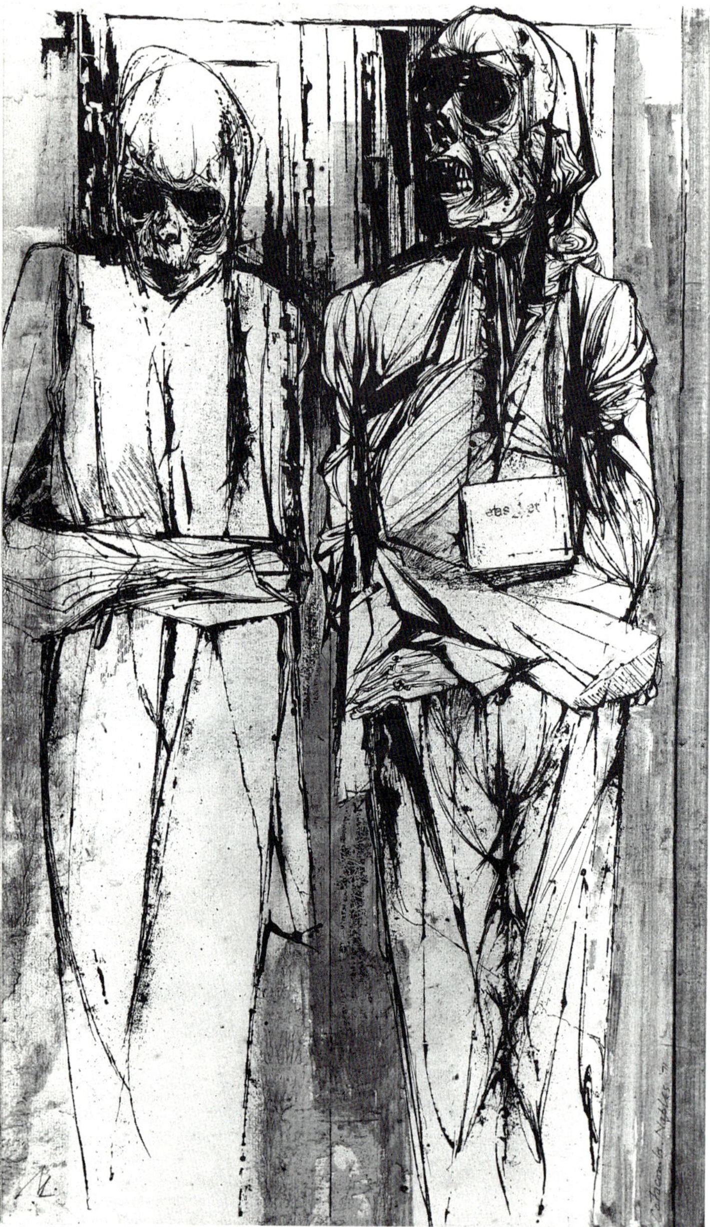

49 Female Scarecrow: Fantasy early 1970s

Black ink, traces of pastel, paper subsequently laminated
760 x 495 mm
Signed lower l: Nigel Lambourne, undated
[Part of the imagery derived over many years – however remotely – from *Dog Years* by Günter Grass]
Nigel Lambourne Estate

50 An die Vogelscheuche early 1970s

Pen and ink
765 x 560 mm
signed lower l: Nigel Lambourne, undated
inscribed r: an die Vogelscheuche [from *Dog Years* by Günter Grass]
Nigel Lambourne Estate

51 Doll Fantasy (ii) early 1970s

Acrylic wash in 2 tones of turquoise and 2 of grey on smooth hardboard, pencil, black and white chalks and touches of pink body colour
725 x 440 mm
Signed lower l and centre r edge in pencil with lower signature overwritten in ink: Nigel Lambourne, not dated
[An uncharacteristic venture into colour, on themes developed after he knew both Kleist's writing and Hans Bellmer's pictures]
Private collection

52 Scene from Marlowe's 'Dr Faustus' c.1970

Black pen and wash
510 x 370 mm
Signed lower l: Nigel Lambourne, not dated
[A trial lithograph was made from this drawing in 1971 by the Leipziger Presse for a projected illustrated edition of the play which failed to go ahead]
Private collection

53 Catacombs, Naples 1971

Black pen and wash on grey paper
560 x 340 mm
Signed lower l: NL
Titled edge r: Catacombs. Naples '71
Private collection

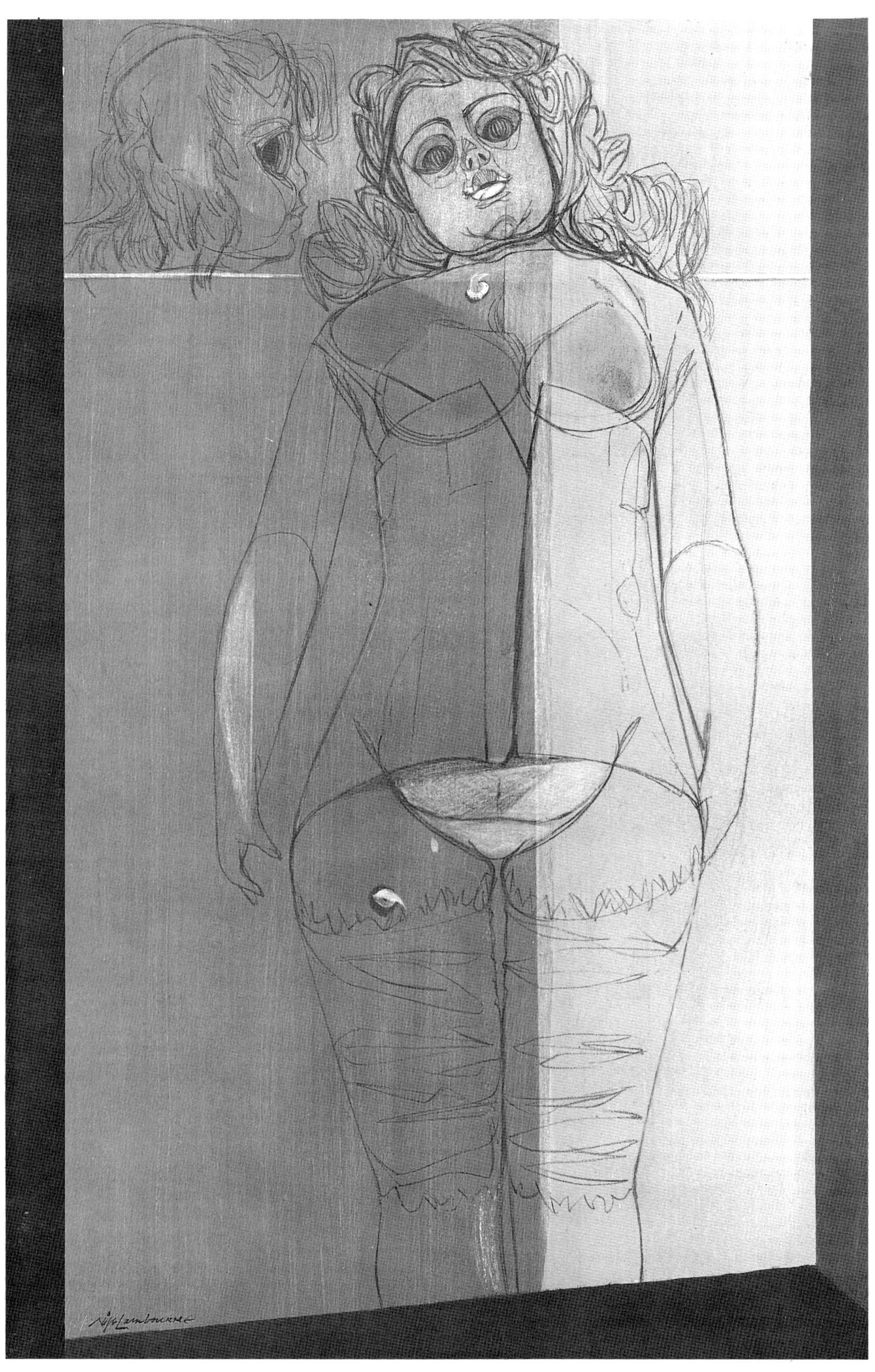

[No. 51] *Doll Fantasy (ii)*

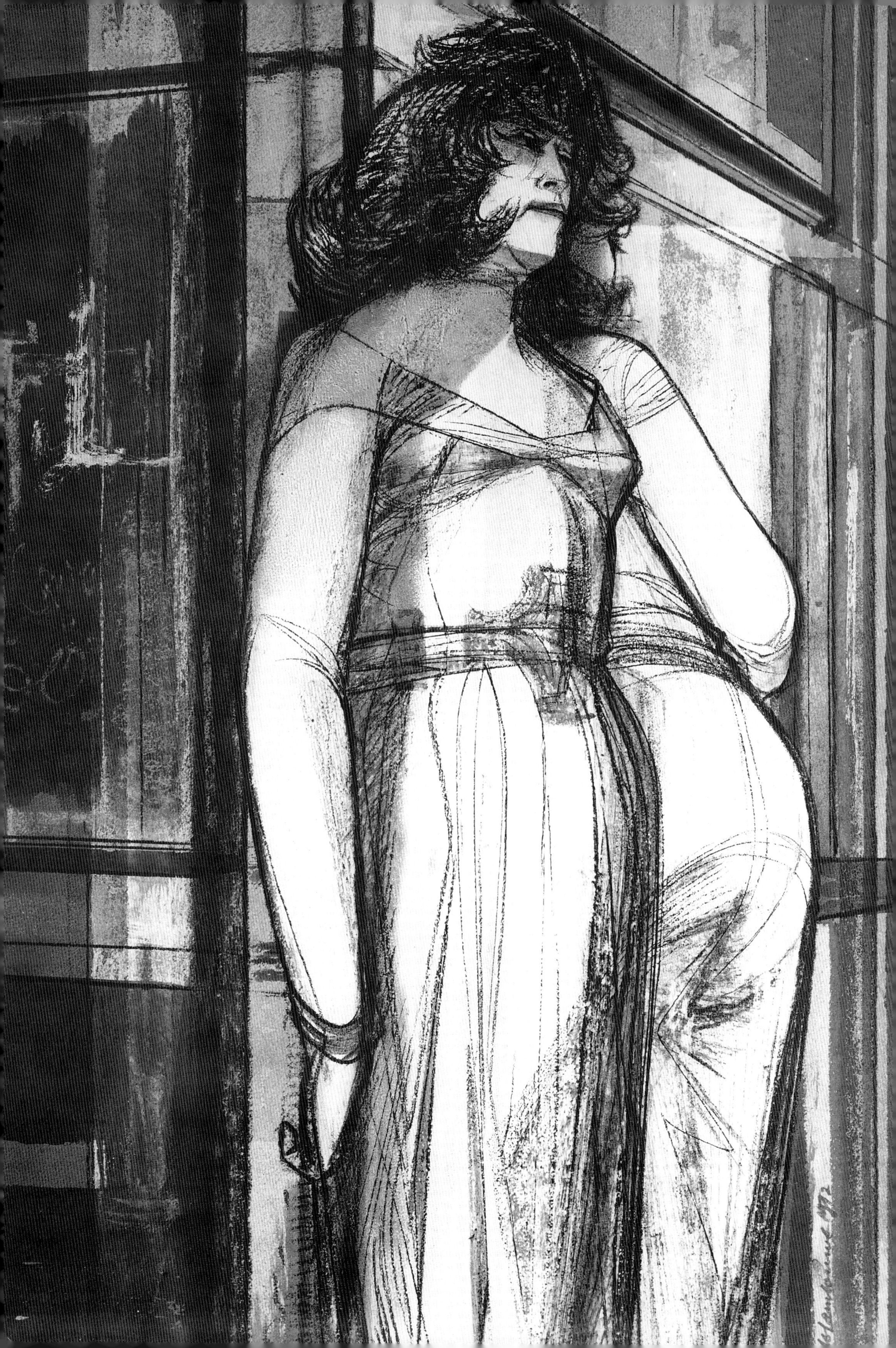

54 **Rue Mozart, Marseille** 1972

Chalk and watercolour
630 x 445 mm
Signed lower edge r: Nigel Lambourne 1972
Inscribed: Rue Mozart, Marseille
Nigel Lambourne Estate

55 **Students' Concert** 1972/74

Black chalk with yellow, brown and blue-grey washes
715 x 495 mm
Signed lower l: Nigel Lambourne
Titled lower edge l: 'Students' Concert', 1972/74
[Also exists in a linocut version, 47]
Private collection

56 **Lovers** 1974 or earlier

Linocut
460 x 320 mm
Signed lower l: 9/xii, lower r: Nigel Lambourne
Inscribed lower l: for Doug & Sue, Dec. 1974
Private collection

57 **Strip Entertainer** 1974 or earlier

Pen and indian ink
545 x 370 mm
Unsigned, not dated
Private collection

58 **Entertainer** 1974

Indian ink, pastel and watercolour
520 x 365 mm
Signed lower l: Nigel Lambourne, '74
Nigel Lambourne Estate

59 **Figure Dressing** c.1975

Pencil, black and white chalks and pen on grey paper
665 x 450 mm
Signed lower l: Nigel Lambourne May '75 (or '76?)
Inscribed lower l: for Bobbie
Nigel Lambourne Estate

[No. 54] *Rue Mozart, Marseille*

60 **Turkish Cemetery** [ii] c.1976

Pen and ink
550 x 425 mm
Signed: Nigel Lambourne, undated
Inscribed on back of frame: Turkish Cemetery [ii]
[Turkish Cemetery (i) is dated 1976, and both drawings may have been developed from sketch material dating from the visits of 1964/5]
Nigel Lambourne Estate

61 **Scene V: from Marlowe's 'Dr Faustus'** 1976

Black pen and wash
435 x 245 mm
Signed lower r: N. L. '76
Titled lower r: Scene V: Dr Faustus imagines a Wife 'a Devil as a Woman.'
Private collection

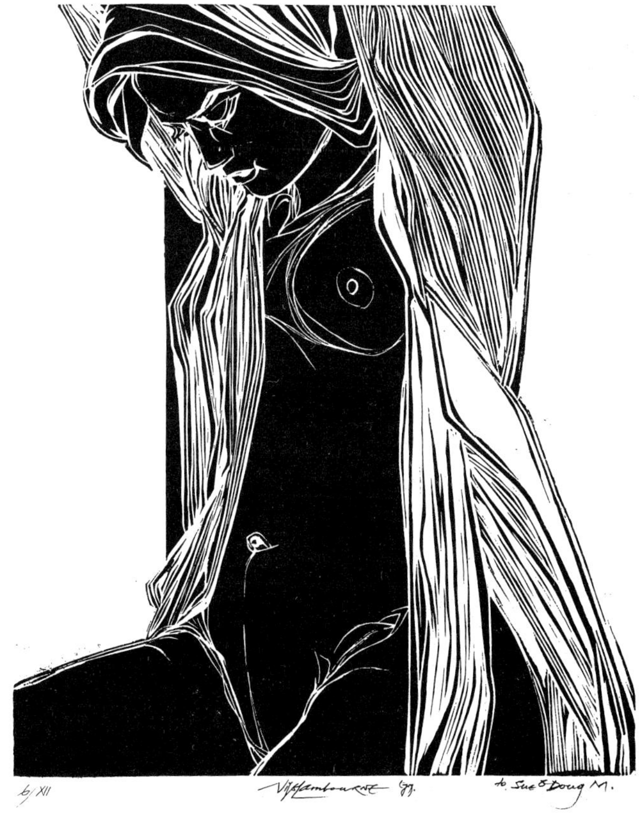

[No. 65] *Seated Figure in Nightdress*

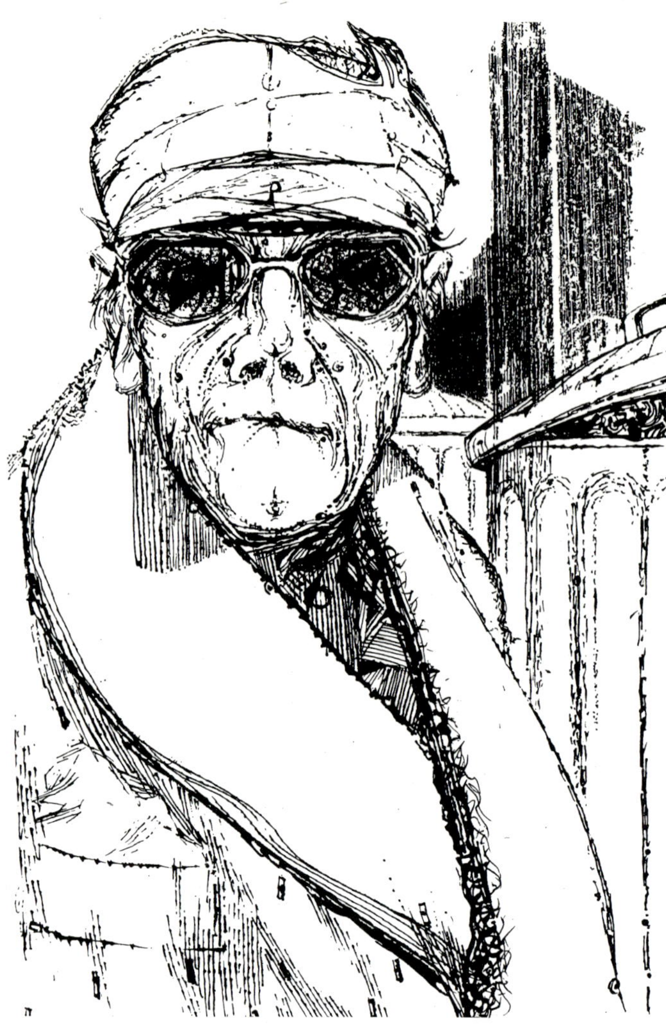

[No. 64] *Endgame (Samuel Beckett)*

62 Scene VIII: from Marlowe's 'Dr Faustus' 1976

Black pen and wash
420 x 270 mm
Signed in lower part of drawing: N. L., not dated, untitled
Private collection

63 Scarecrow Pair 1976

Pen and ink
660 x 460 mm
Signed lower r: Nigel Lambourne
'Hundejahre' No. 1
Inscribed lower l: for B, anniversaire, July '76
Nigel Lambourne Estate

64 Endgame (Samuel Beckett) 1976

Pen and indian ink
230 x 155 mm
Unsigned, not dated
[Commissioned for the Haymarket Theatre, Leicester]
Private collection

65 Seated Figure in Nightdress 1977

Linocut
340 x 280 mm
Signed Nigel Lambourne '77
Inscribed: 6/xii, to Sue & Doug M.
Private collection

66 Ovid's 'Amores' c.1977

Unpublished book illustration
Woodcut
106 x 106 mm
Unsigned artist's proof, initialled NL in the block, not dated
Private collection

67 Seated, Looking Left 1970s

Chalk drawing
665 x 500 mm
No signature or date
Nigel Lambourne Estate

[No. 63] *Scarecrow Pair*

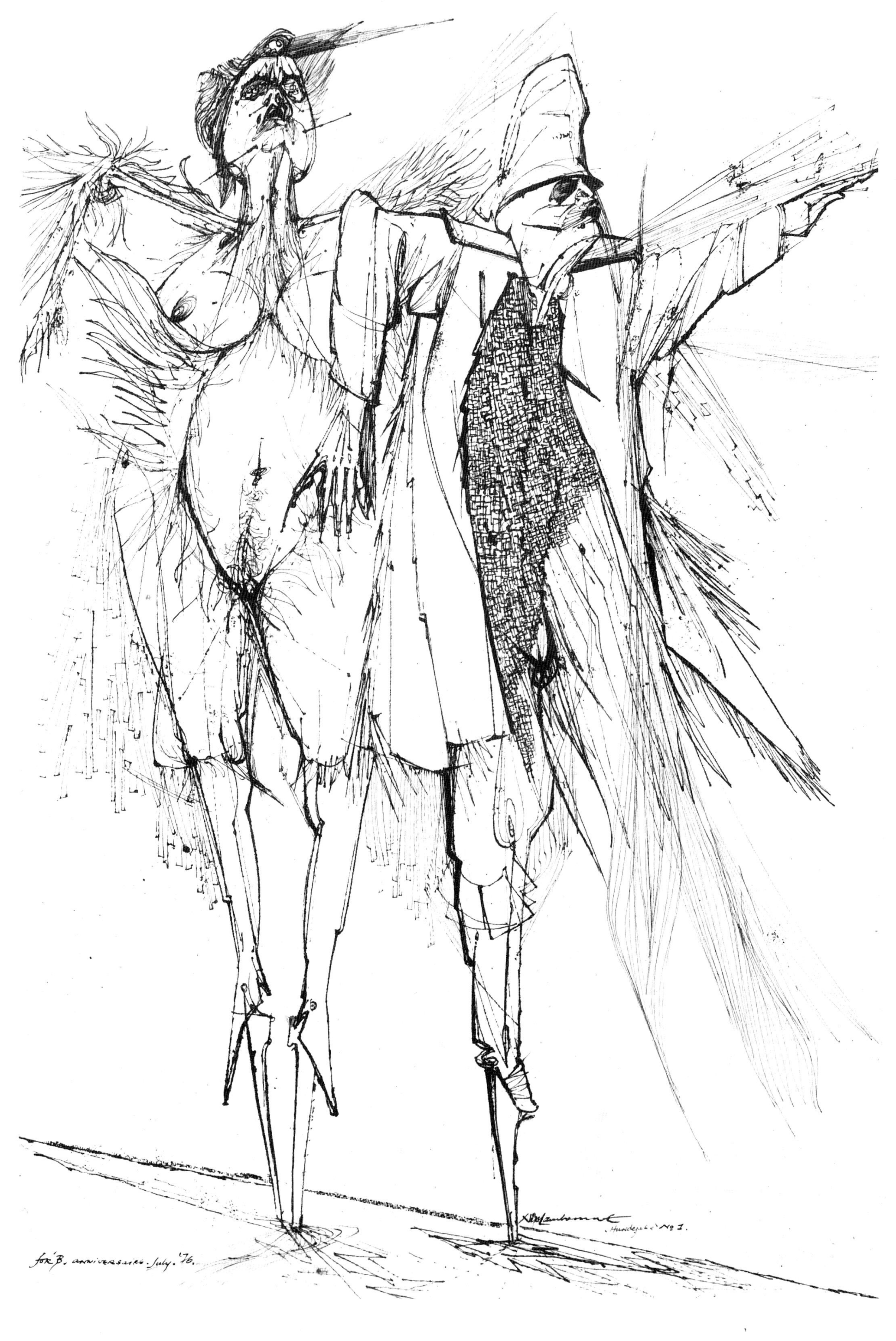
No 1.
for B. anniversaire. July. '76.

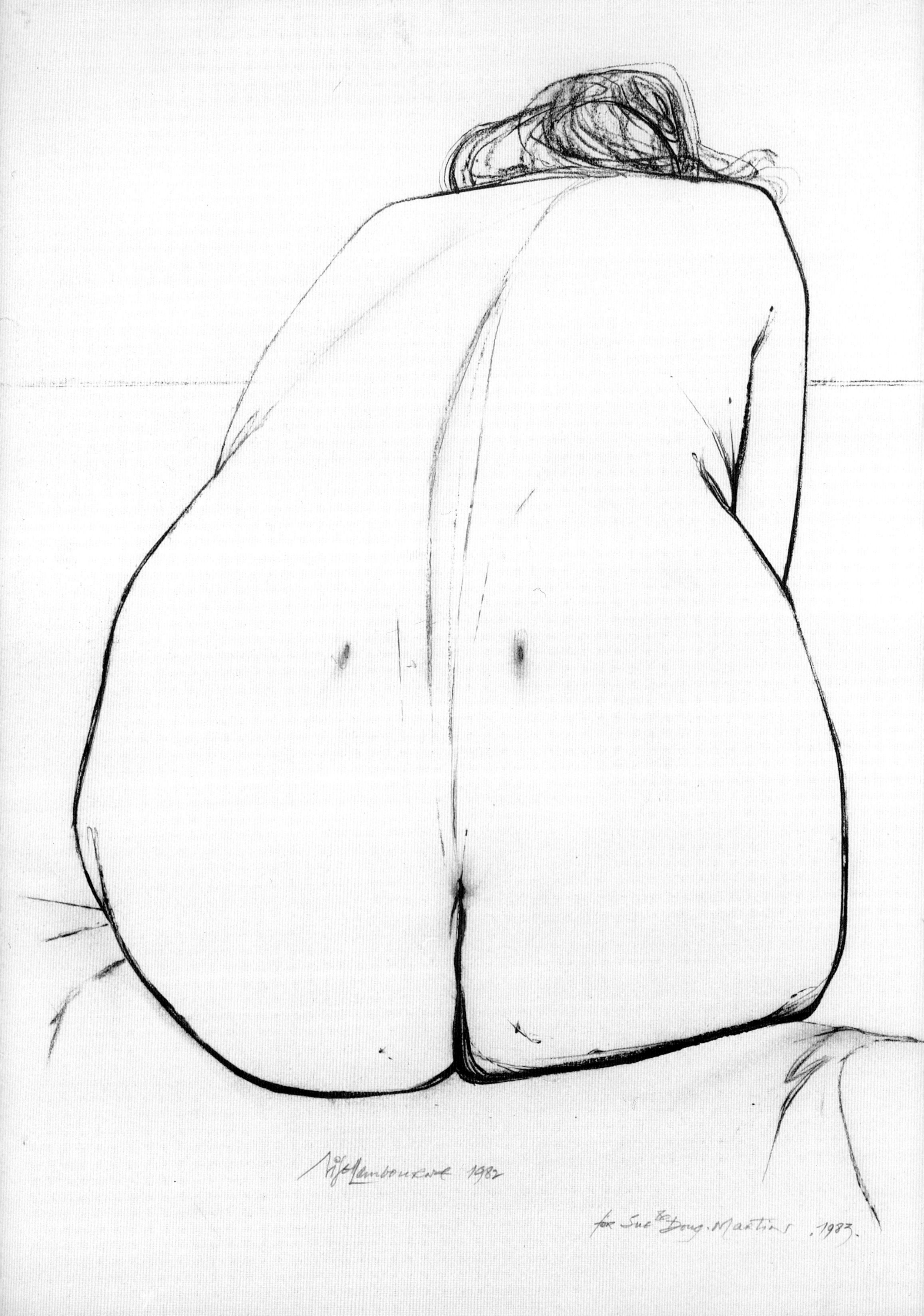
for Sue & Doug. Martins .1983.

68 **Geraldine McEwan** 1970s

Pen and ink and conté crayon
620 x 280 mm
Signed lower r: Nigel Lambourne, undated
Inscribed lower l: Geraldine McEwan, Webster, 'The White Devil'
Nigel Lambourne Estate

69 **At a Beach Hut Door [ii]** 1970s

Chalk, pencil, pastel and wash
745 x 535 mm
Signed lower r: Nigel Lambourne, undated
Inscribed: at a Beach Hut Door ii
Nigel Lambourne Estate

70 **Nightdress [iii]** 1980

Black, terracotta and white chalk with grey pastel on grey paper
635 x 405 mm
Signed lower edge r: Nigel Lambourne May '80
Titled lower l: Nightdress iii
[An earlier version of this same composition, 'Undressing' (1969), in pastel, chalk and ink was shown at the Belgrave Gallery]
Private collection

71 **Lovers** 1980

Gouache, lift ground, aquatint (copper) print
355 x 275 mm
Signed below: iv/9 Nigel Lambourne '80
Private collection

72 **Life Study** 1982

Pencil, brown and black chalks
525 x 455 mm
Signed below: Nigel Lambourne 1982
Inscribed beneath: for Sue & Doug Martin 1983
Private collection

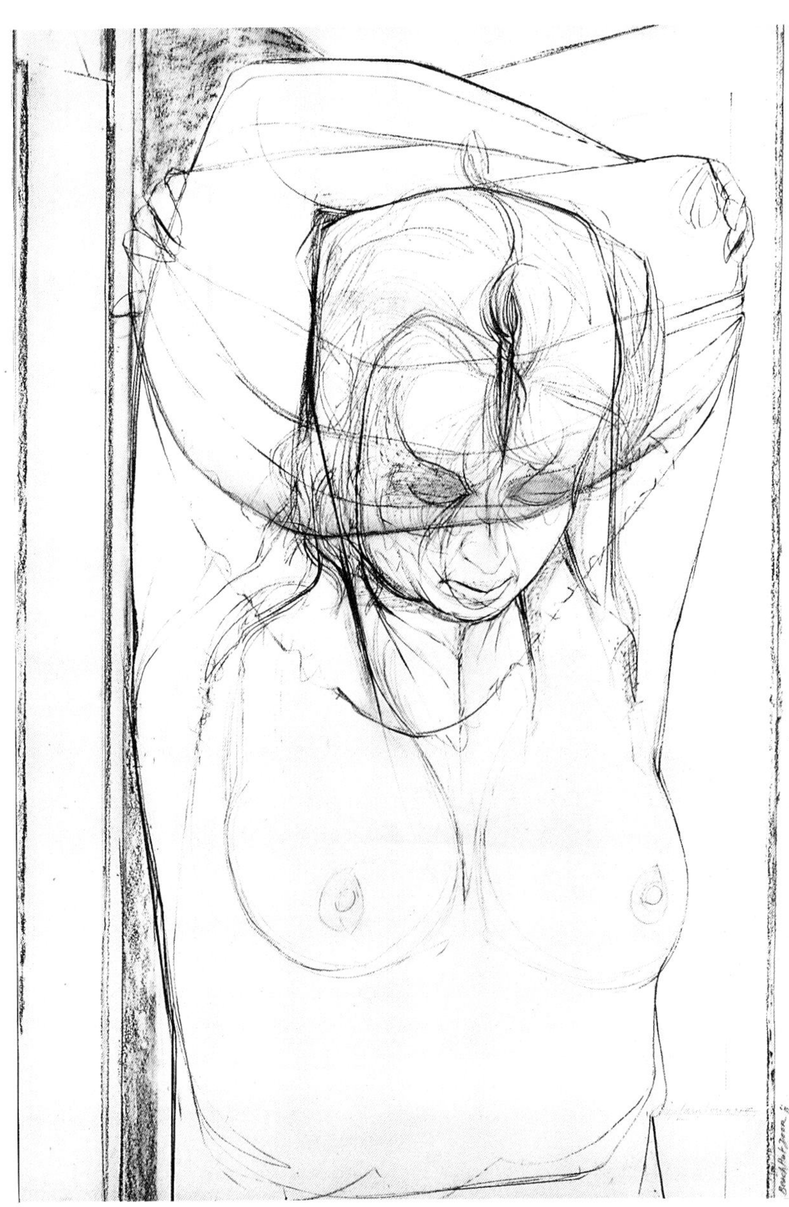

73 Standing Woman with Arms behind Head
1984 or earlier

Linocut
460 x 215 mm
Unnumbered artist's proof, signed in block: NL
Signed: Nigel Lambourne 1984
Private collection

74 Torso for the Sake of It 1986

Chalk, pen and brush drawing in blue-grey, brown and black
575 x 355 mm
Signed lower r: Nigel Lambourne, '86
Titled lower edge r: torso for the sake of it
Private collection

75 Diagram of a Torso, Maybe? 1988

Grey and terracotta chalk and olive green pen line
535 x 345 mm
Signed lower r: Nigel Lambourne '88
[His final recorded drawing]
Private collection

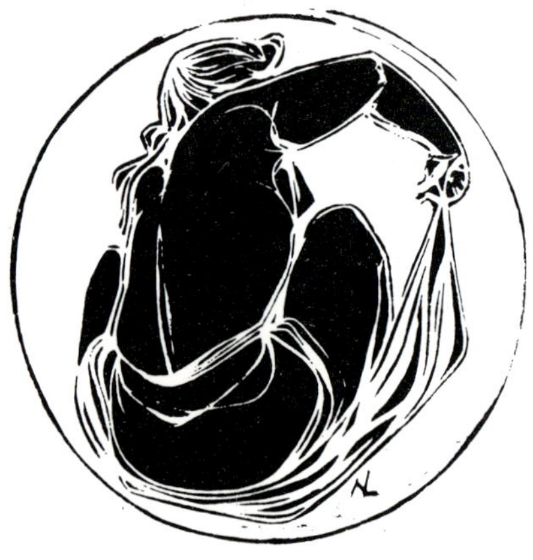

[No. 66] *Ovid's 'Amores'*